# Theos – clear thinking on religion

Theos is the UK's leading religion and society think tank. With our ide[...] combined circulation of 160 million in the past 10 years, we are shapi[...] about the role of faith in contemporary society by means of high quality research, events and media commentary. We provide a credible, informed and gracious Christian voice in our mainstream public conversations.

*The Economist* calls us "an organisation that demands attention", and Julian Baggini, the influential atheist philosopher, has said "Theos provides rare proof that theology can be interesting and relevant even – perhaps especially – for those who do not believe."

To learn more, check us out on social media:

twitter.com/theosthinktank | facebook.com/theosthinktank | www.theosthinktank.co.uk

## Why we exist

Religion has emerged as one of the key public issues of the 21st century, both nationally and globally. Our increasingly religiously-diverse society demands that we grapple with religion as a significant force in public life. Unfortunately, much of the debate about the role and place of religion has been unnecessarily emotive and ill-informed. We exist to change that.

We reject the notion of any possible 'neutral' perspective on these issues. We also reject the idea that religion is a purely private matter or that it is possible to divide public and private values for anyone.

We seek, rather, to recognise and analyse the ethical ideas and commitments that underlie public life and to engage in open and honest public debate, bringing the tradition of Christian social and political thought to bear on current issues. We believe that the mainstream Christian tradition has much to offer for a flourishing society.

## What we do

Theos conducts research, publishes reports, and holds debates, seminars and lectures on the intersection of religion, politics and society in the contemporary world. We also provide regular comment for print and broadcast media and briefing and analysis to parliamentarians and policy makers. To date, Theos has produced over 50 research reports focusing on the big issues impacting British society, including welfare (*The Future of Welfare: A Theos Collection*), law (*"Speaking Up" – Defending and Delivering Access to Justice Today*), economics (*Just Money: How Catholic Social Teaching can Redeem Capitalism*), multiculturalism (*Making Multiculturalism Work*) and voting reform (*Counting on Reform*), as well as on a range of other religious, legal, political and social issues.

In addition to our independently-driven work, Theos provides research, analysis and advice to individuals and organisations across the private, public and not-for-profit sectors. Our staff and consultants have strong public affairs experience, an excellent research track record and a high level of theological literacy. We are practised in research, analysis, debate, and media relations.

## Where we sit

We are committed to the traditional creeds of the Christian faith and draw on social and political thought from a wide range of theological traditions. We also work with many non-Christian and non-religious individuals and organisations.

Theos was launched with the support of the Archbishop of Canterbury and the Cardinal Archbishop of Westminster, but it is independent of any particular denomination. We are an ecumenical Christian organisation, committed to the belief that religion in general and Christianity in particular has much to offer for the common good of society as a whole. We are not aligned with any point on the party political spectrum, believing that Christian social and political thought cuts across these distinctions.

# Join the discussion by becoming a Friend of Theos

## Impact how society views Christianity and shape the cultural debate

The Friends' Programme is designed specifically for people who wish to enter the heart of the current debate. When you join, our commitment is to keep you informed, equipped, encouraged and inspired so that you can be a voice in the public square with us.

## As a member of the Friends' Programme, you are provided with:

- *Hard copies of all our latest reports* on the most pressing issues – social justice, welfare, politics, spirituality, education, money, atheism, humanism…
- *Free access to our events.* Theos hosts a number of high calibre speakers (e.g. Rowan Williams, Larry Siedentop, Grace Davie) and debates ('Magna Carta and the future of liberty', 'Does humanism need Christianity?'). As a friend, you will receive invitations to all these without charge.
- *A network of like-minded people* who wish to share ideas and collaborate with one another. We host networking events which help you meet fellow Friends and build your own network, allowing ideas to flow and connections to form.
- *Our monthly e-newsletter* which is your one-stop digest for the latest news regarding religion and society.
- **If you join as an Associate,** you are *invited to private functions with the team*, allowing you to discuss upcoming projects, review the latest issues and trends in society, and have your say in where you see the public debate is going.

You can become a Friend or Associate today by visiting our website
www.theosthinktank.co.uk

If you'd prefer additional information, you can write to us directly:
Friends Programme, Theos, 77 Great Peter Street, London, SW1P 2EZ

If you have any inquiries regarding the Programme, you can email us at:
friends@theosthinktank.co.uk

# Doing Good: A Future for Christianity in the 21st Century

Nick Spencer

With a foreword by

Justin Welby, Archbishop of Canterbury

Vincent Nichols, Archbishop of Westminster

Published by Theos in 2016
© Theos

ISBN 978-0-9931969-7-3

Some rights reserved – see copyright licence for details
For further information and subscription details please contact:

Theos
Licence Department
77 Great Peter Street
London
SW1P 2EZ

T 020 7828 7777
E hello@theosthinktank.co.uk
www.theosthinktank.co.uk

# contents

Strange things are happening to Christianity in the United Kingdom.

While critics prophesy its imminent demise – as critics have done for several hundred years – Christians across the country are doing what they, too, have done for many hundreds of years: worship, pray, witness, serve.

There is nothing, of course, strange about this. What is strange – or at least worthy of greater notice than it usually receives – is that the breadth, depth and intensity of this Christian service is deepening. From personal debt advice to marriage counselling, from foodbanks to street pastors, from rehabilitation to reconciliation, the Church and Christian charities across the country are rolling up their sleeves, struggling on behalf of human dignity, pursuing the common good – and doing it all in the name of Jesus Christ.

What makes this profoundly practical and deeply spiritual service all the more interesting is that it is happening in a national landscape that is itself undergoing significant changes. Periods of predominance of the state or, alternatively, of the market, have revealed the weakness of both, sometimes with dire consequences. Increasingly, politicians and commentators across the political spectrum are realising that a good society desperately needs a third element if it is to be truly healthy.

This element, sometimes known as civil society, is one in which people come together and serve simply for the sake of service, recognising a common humanity. It is an element in which the Church has long dwelt and one in which it continues today to demonstrate the unquenchable love of God on an enormous scale.

In 2006, our predecessors as Archbishops of Canterbury and Westminster, Rowan Williams and Cormac Murphy O'Connor, welcomed the launch of the think tank Theos. We have watched closely and admired its rigorous and thoughtful work over the last ten years, and are delighted to commend this ten year anniversary report.

In it, Nick Spencer charts a view of the future for Christianity in the UK, drawing on the wealth of data and evidence that Theos has accumulated in its years of research. That view is one in which service is central, but it is *service-as-witness*, service that is firmly rooted in, shaped by and unashamed of its faith in Jesus Christ. The report's idea of "Christian social liturgy" expresses how Christians can combine their fidelity to the two greatest commandments – loving God and loving their neighbour – in a way that is simultaneously distinctive and inclusive.

Ultimately, the future of Christianity in the United Kingdom – as, of course, everywhere – rests in the hands of God, who raised Jesus Christ from the dead. For this reason we are firmly convinced that as Christians seek to embody the love of Christ in their service across the country, that future is one about which we can be full of hope.

The Most Revd Justin Welby
Archbishop of Canterbury

Cardinal Vincent Nichols
Archbishop of Westminster

December 2016

On 3 May 2016 the BBC Radio 4 programme *You and Yours* looked at the issue of 'Debt and Mental Health' problems. Both of these, separately and together, are an increasing problem in UK society, and the programme took calls from listeners who had experienced them, and connected them with counsellors and money experts who gave them advice.

Towards the end of the programme, they took a call from a 68-year old woman whose situation was, in her own words, "horrendous". She had major debt problems due to her husband's longstanding paranoid schizophrenia. Unbeknown to her, he had accumulated over £20,000 of debt through various channels to pay for his gambling addiction. He didn't work, and they were now afraid to answer the phone or open the post. The result was not only poverty and fear but a radically-broken marital relationship, in which, she said, she felt more like a mother or debt-policer than a wife. "It's affected how we love one another", she remarked with painful honesty.

Martin Lewis, the independent money saving expert listened to her and tried to offer some reassurance. He said that in many instances of major hidden debts he suggested visiting a non-profit debt counselling service but, in his words, "you're beyond that." He then went on to say, "I would say that the right organisation for you is a wonderful organisation called CAP UK, which is Christians Against Poverty." "You don't have to be a Christian," he reassured her. Christianity was what inspired them, "why they do it", not who they do it for or to.

CAP UK, he went on, was different from other debt counsellors. Citizens Advice, Step Change, National Debt Line were all very good agencies, he explained, but they were "functional", like an accountant who sort out your financial problems. "What CAP UK do is they come to the house, give you many more hours and they also do emotional counselling to do with the debt counselling... I think you could do with someone who comes around, makes you a cup of tea, holds your hands, talks through this, and gets the money sorted out at the same time... I hear wonderful things about people who've been to them."

This painful but hopeful exchange offers a neat summary of what this essay, written to mark ten years of the Christian think tank, Theos, is about.

Theos was launched in November 2006 with an essay entitled *"Doing God"*, a phrase that was then even more popular than it is today. Its subtitle went on to explain that it was focused on the "future for faith in the public square", and proceeded to explore the reasons against this kind of 'doing God', to respond to these and to argue that we would hear a great deal more about God in public life over the coming years.

Ten years on the temptation to revisit the original arguments within *"Doing God"* is limited. The arguments for and against remain more or less the same, and while some of the trends identified have faded,[1] other 'trends', such as the Arab Spring and its ensuing Christian Winter, have emerged and grown.

For that reason, this anniversary essay takes a slightly different approach, focusing not on generic 'faith' – never an ideal term – or on religion in general, but on Christianity specifically.

There are two reasons for this. First, although one can't talk about different religions without talking about 'religion' (the latter term cropping up several times in the ensuing pages), the whole debate around faith and religion in contemporary Britain suffers from what one might call "terminological inexactitude" – and not just in the tongue-in-cheek sense of 'a lie' in which Churchill first used the phrase. Quite apart from the dubiously 'essentialist' assumptions behind the word itself – there are lots of religions but is there such a thing as religion? – the category is worryingly capacious. In effect, any term that encompasses both the Quakers and ISIS is unlikely to do much fine analytical work. Looking at Christianity specifically affords a degree of specificity to a debate that is beset with nervous ambiguities.

Second, Christianity faces challenges in contemporary Britain that it has not experienced in living memory, arguably ever. This essay does not shy away from the numbers games, which it paints in lurid technicolour in the opening chapter. Talking about Christianity rather than 'religion' or 'faith' allows us to put some empirical flesh on theoretical bones (although how much and how accurately is a moot point, as the lengthy footnotes in chapter one explain). But it also affords an opportunity to place those details in their proper context, which is too rarely done, and to think carefully about what they mean and what should be done.

So it is that this tenth anniversary essay, explores a future (not *the* future) for Christianity in a country that has been incalculably shaped by its concerns[2] but which has, at best, a somewhat ambiguous relationship with that particular faith at the moment. That future, it concludes, lies in the kind of 'Christian social liturgy' (the phrase is explained later on) exemplified by the exchange on *You and Yours*: the open, authentic and maybe even distinctive practical manifestation of the love of God.

In that instance it was a debt advice agency that understands the indebted (and their loved ones) as *persons*, recognising the need for fully human service – meaning not only providing expert advice but also coming along side and 'being with' the person as a fellow, fallible human – and providing it inclusively without ever hiding the fact that the motivation for doing so is the love of Christ. In other instances, it might be organisations providing a practical and pastoral support to often troubled night life in British towns and cities (as with Street Pastors[3]/City Angels[4]); giving the opportunity for people with and without severe learning disabilities to share their life and work together in a way that reveals the profound but vulnerable humanity of both (as with L'Arche[5]); or offering spiritual, practical and emotional support to the homeless in Brighton & Hove (as with Off the Fence[6]). Whatever it is, the future of Doing God in the UK, the essay argues, will be inextricably linked to the practice of Doing Good.

This very statement will unnerve some people. On the one hand, it may convey a certain understanding of social action which is professionalised and impersonal, in which experts deliver goods to those in need. On the other, it may convey memories of the kind of 'Social Gospel' which, earlier in the 20th century, did much good work but often ended up retaining the 'social' while jettisoning the 'gospel'.

The phrase is intended to avoid both of those impressions. In the first instance, 'Doing Good' is more a matter of coming alongside and 'dwelling with' other people, not as technocratic experts (though in some circumstances professional expertise will be important), still less as people whose own lives are fully sorted, but rather as people who are themselves disciples, or 'learners' – alert to their own fallibility and need for love and healing. 'Doing Good' is not a matter of delivering services to users so much as developing mutual service between persons; not 'fixing' poverty, or problems, or people, but building relationships of common care that recognise, humanise and heal.[7]

In the second instance, the idea of 'Doing Good' is steered away from old-school social gospel in the final chapter by an idea that the essay calls 'social liturgy', a deliberate marriage of 'Christian social action' and 'priestly service'. To get to this point, however, the essay takes a rocky path through the reality of Christianity and of society in contemporary Britain.

Chapter one looks at what has happened to Christianity in the UK over the last decade or so. The picture is a sobering one (at least for Christians). Although not as precipitous or monolithic as some imagine, the story is one of (much) lower levels of affiliation combined with (slightly) lower levels of attendance, albeit attenuated by changing temporal, geographical and denominational patterns. In essence, the shift is in 'nominalism' – from 'Christian' having once been the default identity option for people born in the UK, to 'no religion' today. In itself that doesn't say anything about belief or behaviour, but it is nonetheless a significant cultural shift to which we should pay attention.

The chapter proceeds to explain how this big story mixes with other stories, such as attendance (in as far as we can tell, down slightly on ten years ago), different patterns of attendance, the rise of non-religiosity and of Islam as significant identity and belief markers, and, more widely still, the global trends pertaining to 'religion' and religiosity, where, as sociologist Peter Berger once remarked, the world is as furiously religious as ever it was. Chapter one will not make for cheery reading for those bothered about the future of Christianity in the UK, but if Christ is the way and "the truth" those who follow him have a duty to listen to the truth even – especially – when it hurts.

Chapter two pulls the camera wider in trying to make the often-overlooked link between the Christian faith and the society in which it has its being – between, as it were, the data in chapter one and the response in chapter three. It begins with the key fact that discussions of Christian trends in Britain often focus exclusively on how many people believe X or attend Y or affiliate with Z. None of these facts is immaterial, but the problem is that an exclusive focus on them is in danger of treating Christianity as if it were just a set of beliefs or a club. In his Bishop Paddock Memorial lectures, delivered a century ago, the young William Temple quoted an "eminent politician" who is said to have remarked that the church was "a voluntary organisation for the maintenance of public worship in the interest of those who desire to join it". Temple protested vigorously, as we might today: looking at the past, present or future of Christianity simply by measuring attendance or affiliation or belief figures detaches it from any sense of "life to the full" or of the true meaning of Kingdom of God that Jesus came preaching. Evangelism, for example, is not the business of persuading people to give up an hour every Sunday morning in order to get into heaven, or of backing them into a corner and proving the propositional content of the creeds till they wither and submit, but, as Temple's most recent successor as Archbishop of Canterbury, Justin Welby, has said, it is the business of

> showing others – through our words, actions, attitudes and interactions – how God has offered every one of us a new start… [work that] requires us to consider, in every new situation, how we can show others they are loved by God.[8]

This is the foundation for the second chapter. By drawing on the work of Canadian philosopher Charles Taylor, chapter two seeks to put the present situation of Christianity in a wider social context, spiritual and temporal. Regarding the former, although the chapter is clear that for some people religious belief feels genuinely irrelevant and

*These various trends point towards where the future of Christianity in the UK lies – engaging the deep-rooted human curiosity in 'things eternal' through the demonstration of love in 'things temporal'.*

inconsequential, for the majority the loss of Christian identity has been replaced not with atheistic certainty but rather with an amorphous and personalised spirituality. Regarding the latter, it argues that for all the UK remains a comparatively wealthy, comfortable and good place to live, there are pockets, and perhaps even submerged seas, of loneliness, pain, confusion and despair that cry out for attention. Put together, these various trends point towards where the future of Christianity in the UK lies – engaging the deep-rooted human curiosity in 'things eternal' through the demonstration of love in 'things temporal'. Christianity has a word for this – incarnation – but not many people know what that means today.

Chapter three explores a little of what this approach might mean and how it might answer some of the stubborn questions about 'religion' in the public square today. It begins by showing that the one trend pertaining to Christianity in contemporary Britain that runs against the narrative of decline is that of 'social action'. In as far as we have data to show for it, the level of this, both formally and informally, has risen considerably over the last ten years. There may be fewer people on pews but there are many more running luncheon clubs, and mums and toddlers' groups, and foodbanks, and homeless charities, and debt advice centres, and drop-in centres, and the like. Christians are 'doing good'.

As already noted, there is a danger in this approach, of which many will be painfully aware. The movement known as the 'Social Gospel', which flourished in the early years of the 20th century, sought to embody Christian faith in social action in such a way as would simultaneously reform society and establish the Kingdom of God. It was an intelligent, impressive, authentic, and faithful movement but one that declined and fell, in part because the gospel at its heart was eclipsed by the social activism it spawned. There is a salutary warning here, which is why the final chapter introduces and talks about *social liturgy*, rather than social action.

*Social liturgy is a simultaneous expression of love of God and of neighbour, a way of worshipping God through finding and serving him in others.*

This is an (deliberately) unfamiliar phrase. The word liturgy is commonly understood to mean 'church worship' but in reality, the New Testament Greek word from which it derives, *leitourgia*, could be used to mean both priestly service within the Temple *and* public charitable activity. In this context, social liturgy is adopted to capture the idea of charitable public action that is also priestly, or directed immediately at the divine.

Social liturgy is a simultaneous expression of love of God and of neighbour, a way of worshipping God through finding and serving him in others. The essay uses the term in order to underline that the proposed way forward is not simply a return to the admirable but ultimately discredited methods of the social gospel movement of the past. Rather, social liturgy is just another way of worshipping God in public.

Chapter three argues that it is this kind of 'Doing Good' by which we will Do God in the 21st century. It outlines what social liturgy might involve and then engages with a number of genuine and serious objections (or at least hesitations) concerning this, arguing that the idea speaks to a number of key concerns pertaining to the 'problems' of proselytism, pluralism, public legitimacy, and public reasoning.

Ultimately, the future of Christianity in the UK is uncertain and clearly in a moment of some flux. But there are good reasons, and specifically reasons to do with what we identify as 'good' today, to believe that the reports of its death have been greatly exaggerated – or perhaps that reports of its death have ignored the fainter rumours of its resurrection.

# introduction – references

1   The well-being agenda, for example, petered out somewhat on account of the crash of 2008-09, while the Big Society idea flourished with the vigour and brevity of the mayfly.

2   For an idea of how much, see Nick Spencer, *Freedom and Order: History, Politics and the English Bible* (Hodder, 2012) and *The Evolution of the West: How Christianity shaped our values* (SPCK, 2016).

3   http://www.streetpastors.org/

4   http://www.cityangels.org.uk/

5   http://www.larche.org.uk/

6   http://www.offthefence.org.uk/

7   I am grateful to Bethany Eckley of Church Urban Fund for helping steer and clarify my thinking on this matter.

8   http://www.archbishopofcanterbury.org/pages/evangelism.html

# bad news about the good news

## brace yourselves

The Sunday after Theos was founded there were approximately 4.5 million people in church in the UK.[1] That figure comprised around 1.1 million Anglicans, 1.2 million Catholics and 2.2 million from other denominations.[2] Next Sunday, assuming you are reading this essay in 2016 or thereabouts, it is likely to be approximately 4.2 million, comprising 1 million Anglicans, 1 million Catholics and 2.2 million others.[3]

That is a hard truth from which Christians, and those sympathetic towards the Christian faith, cannot shy away.[4] Church attendance is not the be-all-and-end-all of the Christian life. There are worthwhile debates to be had about what attendance actually signifies (what level of commitment, for example); how patterns of attendance are changing (as the British weekend changes); and whether 'attendance' today means the same thing as attendance in yesteryear (it almost certainly does not). But as a basic litmus test of the level of practical, rather than notional, commitment to the Christian faith, it is pretty good and therefore, for Christians, pretty discouraging.

It is primarily from church attendance figures, and particularly Church of England attendance figures, that the now well-entrenched 'narrative of decline' is derived. However, the church attendance figures are only one set of national Christian statistics, and not the most dispiriting either.

The significance of *affiliation* – what religious label people do or do not feel comfortable with – is even more debateable than attendance. Some claim that affiliation is all but meaningless; others that it only becomes meaningful *in extremis*, at 'junction' or 'terminus' points in an individual's life; still others that it is meaningful continually (rather than simply *in extremis*) but only in a low key way.[5] However one interprets affiliation, the fact is that the downward trend in Christian affiliation over the last ten years is more noticeable than that in attendance.

Theos was unhelpfully founded in between censuses, but the figures from 2001 and 2011 give a good indication as to the direction of travel between 2006 and 2016. In 2001, 72%

of people in England and Wales called themselves Christian in the census, 6% were of other religions, and 15% claimed to be of 'No religion'. A decade later these figures were 59%, 11% and 25% respectively. According to the British Social Attitudes (BSA) survey in 2006, 22% of people in Great Britain considered themselves to be Anglican, 9% Roman Catholic and 16% Other Christian. By 2014, the first two figures had fallen to 18% and 8% respectively, while the third had risen to 17%. From having been the kind of thing you instinctively wrote on your Census form (and would have been even more so had the religion question been asked in 1991 or 1981, 'Christian' has become much a label of choice, 'no religion' increasingly becoming the default option).

These two data lines – and the comparison between them – suggest that the main trend of the last decade has been a transfer from Christian – and in particular Anglican – 'nominalism' (using the term to mean those who affiliate with Christianity but do not attend the church) to no-religion. (The BSA no-religion figures increased from 46% to 49% in the intervening time.) The number of 'committed' Christians (meaning, in this instance, those who attend regularly) has dropped but far less sharply than the number of nominals. In other words, ticking the 'Christian' box is no longer the automatic option. We are witnessing the passing of the *default* Christian identity.

> We are witnessing the passing of the default Christian identity.

Whether the non-religiosity to which these nominal Christians have turned is itself 'committed' or 'nominal' – in other words, whether this growing number of non-religious people are 'devout' and dedicated in their rejection of religion, or whether they simply adopt the non-religious label in the way they once adopted the Christian one – is not always easy to tell, for the obvious reason that there are no measures of the non-religious equivalent of 'attendance'. One 2015 study showed that among the non-religious, "only 40% are convinced that there is no God or 'higher power', and 5% of them are absolutely certain that He does exist."[8] Not being committed to a religion is clearly not the same as being committed to non-religiosity (a category error that some non-religious groups repeatedly make).[9] Some indication of the nature of this shift, however, may be gleaned by two disconnected series of data.

> Not being committed to a religion is clearly not the same as being committed to non-religiosity (a category error that some non-religious groups repeatedly make).

The first is on membership levels of specifically non-religious groups, such as local and national atheist, humanist and secularist groups. This is rather hard to come by but it appears to be in the thousands rather than the millions. **Just as British Christianity is disproportionately concentrated in London, non-religious humanism appears to** be concentrated in London and the South East.[10] Unlike London churches, however, membership of the UK's leading anti-religious organisation, the British Humanist Association, was disproportionately male and also fitted closely with its characterisation as a 'middle class intelligentsia',[11] "with 82% of members in 2014 in possession of an undergraduate or postgraduate degree and the overwhelming majority in professional or managerial occupations, especially in education and information technology." For all its considerable cultural clout, therefore, 'committed' non-religiosity in the UK is not an active mass movement.

Second are the data on levels of Christian knowledge and understanding, a topic on which Theos has occasionally conducted polling over the last ten years. In one such survey, in 2008, we found that only 12% of adults in Britain had a good knowledge of the Christmas story.[12] Research by Bible Society found parents' knowledge of 'well-known' Bible stories was poor: asked to decide whether a series of plot lines appeared in the Bible almost half of parents (46%) failed to recognise the plot of Noah's Ark as a Bible story.[13] More substantially, a 2014 study of poll data from 123 national sample surveys of the adult general population and 35 national and local sample surveys of adult religious populations since the Second World War concluded, among other things, that household ownership of the Bible has slumped, readership of the Bible has declined (with only around one in ten reading it at least weekly and three-quarters less than once a year or never), and knowledge of the content was variable but generally low and decreasing.[14]

More recently, and more amusingly, British Religion in Numbers reported on a survey conducted in December 2015 to assess to the knowledge of the general public at Christmas. This found that of the 1,000 children aged 5-12 interviewed, 52% thought Christmas Day was the birthday of Santa Claus, 20% identified Jesus Christ as a footballer with Chelsea FC, 35% believed he was born at the South Pole, and 27% believed he was born in a church.[15] If this particular survey reeks a little of 'amusing Christian news', it is worth remembering that Christmas remains the only widely 'celebrated' Christian festival, and that between them these data are indicative of the general fact, of which few are in doubt: that the level of biblical or Christian knowledge among the British population is not high. This Elizabethan crisis of faith (if it can be called that) is neither the agonised and reluctant turning away we find in Matthew Arnold, James Antony Froude or George Eliot, nor the enraged and indignant rejection we see in Charles Bradlaugh or John Stuart Mill. The Elizabethan public hasn't tasted Christianity and found it wanting, morally, historically or scientifically. Generally speaking, it hasn't tasted Christianity.

> The Elizabethan public hasn't tasted Christianity and found it wanting, morally, historically or scientifically. Generally speaking, it hasn't tasted Christianity.

If these are the headline 'data' stories pertaining to Christianity in contemporary Britain over the last decade, they have jostled with a number of others pertaining to religion, most obviously Islam. While the number of attending Christians has slid in the last decade and the number of nominal Christians has dropped, the number of committed (and affiliated) Muslims has risen.

The 2001 census reported 1.6 million Muslims (or 3% of the population) in England and Wales and this increased to 2.7 million (or 4.5% of the population) by 2011. Although the majority of British Muslims are either immigrants or children of immigrants, there could be, at least according to one study by the University of Swansea, as many as 100,000 Muslim converts in the UK.[16] However precise this figure is – it is somewhat speculative – it is clear that Islam is second only to non-religiosity in terms of growth over the last decade.

Such data have been used to fuel headlines (and fears) about Islam becoming the majority religion in Britain or, more exotically, of the transformation of Europe to Eurabia. Such stories seem ill-founded however, at least in any immediate time frame, and are in part the result of the British population's vastly inflated sense of how many Muslims there are in the UK. When asked "out of every 100 people in Britain, about how many do you think are Muslim?" among those who ventured an opinion (a third did not), 24% (or about five times the actual proportion) was the mean estimate.[17] Such alarmism aside, Islam will undoubtedly play an ever more important role in British public life, either in the problematised guise of security and counter-terrorism that it has over the last decade, or in a more generalised debate over large scale demographics and the speed and nature of social and cultural change.

That recognised, a bigger challenge to Christianity in the UK over coming decades is from its demographic profile, which is disproportionately older than the national average. The age profile of 2011 'Census Christians' (i.e. both nominals *and* practicing Christians) was older than that of all other religious and non-religious groups, with one in five (22%) aged 65 and over.[18] That of practicing Christians is older still, with, for example, two thirds of Church of England worshippers being aged over 55.[19]

> Perhaps churches, and secular societies, are like newspapers: over a certain age people naturally join/purchase them; below that age they satisfy their curiosity and interest through other, more fluid and informal, channels.

It may well be that this is a problem of institutionalisation rather than religiosity *per se* as it is worth noting that organised non-religion seems to suffer from the same ageing problem. According to a 2014-15 study of the British Humanist Association (BHA), nearly two-thirds (65%) of members were aged 50 and over, compared to 38% in that age category from a similar study conducted 50 years earlier, and 35% of the national population.[20] Perhaps churches, and secular societies, are like newspapers: over a certain age people naturally join/purchase them; below that age they satisfy their curiosity and interest through other, more fluid and informal, channels.

Be that as it may, the age profile of practicing Christians in the UK is alarming and, to make matters worse, Christians seem to have far greater problems in 'retaining' their young people than non-religionists do. The National Centre for Social Research's 28th British Social Attitudes survey, in 2011/12, reported that 49% of people brought up as Anglicans retain their Anglican 'identity' (whatever precisely that means) in adulthood. Other Christians (meaning, in effect, other Protestant Christians) report exactly the same figure. Catholics fare slightly better at 63% and non-Christian religions (which because of numbers essentially means Islam) do better still at 87%. But all religious groups are beaten by the retention rate of the non-religious: 94% of children brought up in a non-religious household remain in one.[21]

In one sense, this is simply a refinement of the 'nominalism' data outlined above and is not quite as big a surprise as it may first seem: it merely confirms that Christian and especially Anglican nominalism has much less 'stickiness' in today's culture.[22] Nevertheless, it remains serious if only indicative, and it is easy to see how such data give foundation to the 'extinct within a generation' stories. Still, it does at least suggest that we might think about rewriting, or rather re-ascribing, the famous saying – "Give me the child for his first seven years, and I'll give you the man" – from Jesuits to the non-religious.

> We might think about rewriting, or rather re-ascribing, the famous saying – "Give me the child for his first seven years, and I'll give you the man" – from Jesuits to the non-religious.

## plots and sub-plots

Beginning an essay on the future of Christianity in the UK in such lurid, apocalyptic colours will seem to some readers to be unnecessarily depressing or even at risk of being a self-fulfilling prophecy. However, any essay that seeks to think seriously about the future of Christianity in the UK cannot avoid dealing with the facts, however challenging they may be.

The trends outlined above are indeed challenging but they are not the whole story, and just as it is important to acknowledge difficulties, so it is important to acknowledge complexities. The narrative of Christian decline in the UK is so deeply entrenched that it can be hard to hear any other, and yet there are other stories or, perhaps more accurately, sub-plots which complicate an otherwise comfortably straightforward tale of decline. As David Goodhew has written:

As soon as the discussion moves to whether the British church is in 'net' decline' or 'net' growth, all nuance is lost. The debate becomes a bare-knuckle fight with only two possible results—decline or growth. What if the history of modern British Christianity is much more complex?[23]

It is indeed more complex and the picture of universal, collective, linear decline is a misleading one. Several different sub-plots merit mention. The first is that of regional difference, particularly that of London. According to Peter Brierley's report, *Capital Growth: What the 2012 London Church Census shows*, Sunday church attendance in Greater London rose from 623,000 in 2005 to 722,000 in 2012, while the number of churches in Greater London rose from 4,087 to 4,791 in the same period.[24] London is the clearest example of regional church growth, although Goodhew notes that there are good examples of growth in much of the area within 70 miles of London and indeed in other notable urban areas, such as Birmingham, Edinburgh and Newcastle.[25]

Much of this growth is down to immigration, which offers a second, though closely related, sub-plot. Migrants are disproportionately religious; according to the Pew Forum, of recent migrants to the EU 56% describe themselves as 'Christian,' 27% as 'Muslim,' and 10% as 'non religious'.[26] Not surprisingly, therefore, the growth in British Christianity over the last ten years has been among immigrant communities, there being around 500,000 Christians in black majority churches in Britain and around a million black, Asian, and minority ethnic Christians in Britain.[27] Some of that immigrant growth appears to have been within mainline denominations, Catholic and Anglican. However, much immigrant growth is among the Orthodox and non-mainline denominations, such as Pentecostal and 'New' churches.[28]

These three sub-plots are, in some ways, different perspectives on one major sub-plot, in which immigrants from more Catholic and Anglican countries set up churches in urban areas. In this regard, the judgement of the *Economist* newspaper in 2016 on the future of Christianity in Britain sounds judicious:

> To see the future of Christianity in Britain, go on a Sunday morning to an old Welsh Congregational chapel off the Pentonville Road in Islington. The building has been bought by a Pentecostal Ethiopian church; the congregation raises its hands in a show of unEnglish ecstasy to praise God in Amharic.[29]

The same article goes on to point out, however, that there are other discernible plots.

> A few hours later [in the same chapel], something unexpected happens. A congregation of mainly white members of the Church of England start their

service. This group, known as King's Cross Church, or KXC, has grown from a handful in 2010 to 500 now.

The point is that it is not simply urban, non-white, immigrant churches that are growing. Indeed, according to data from research conducted by Prof. David Voas for the Church of England, although 27% of Church of England parishes are declining, 55% are stable and 18% are actually growing.[30] Similarly, research from the Baptist Union of Britain in 2015 showed that 26% of Baptist churches are growing, and 25% are holding steady.[31] The overall narrative does indeed occlude a significant number of surprisingly different sub-plots.

One final, albeit small, sub-plot is worth mentioning. In 2011/12 Theos and the Grubb Institute conducted a project for the Association of English Cathedrals, looking at the present and future of (Anglican) Cathedrals in England. This was commissioned because it had become clear that cathedral congregations had been on the rise over the previous decade. According to one study on *Cathedrals, Greater Churches and the Growth of the Church*, from October 2013, Anglican cathedrals in England saw overall weekly attendance grow by 35% between 2002 and 2012, while attendance at weekday services more than doubled – from 5,600 to 12,400.[32]

None of these sub-plots change the basic theme of declining affiliation and attendance, but they do suggest that that story is complex as well as challenging.

# bigger picture: religion in the UK

If the picture concerning the Christian presence in contemporary Britain is not a monochrome one, the wider 'religious' context – using that term broadly – complicates matters still further. For all that the UK may be becoming less nominally (and committedly) Christian, it is becoming no less interested in religion; quite the opposite in fact.

When Theos was launched in 2006, the inaugural report quoted an article by the *Guardian*'s then Readers' Editor, Ian Mayes, who was responding to various irate readers who had complained that the paper was covering too much religion. Mayes had gone back through the records and was able to confirm their suspicions that

> there is… more discussion of religion in the pages of the paper… A crude measure is the number of stories in the *Guardian* that mention the word Christian: in 1985, 770; in 1995, 1,221; and in 2005, 2,341. A search for the word Muslim showed: 1985, 408; 1995, 1,106; and in 2005, 2,114.[33]

The trend has continued. In their book, *Media Portrayals of Religion and the Secular Sacred*, Kim Knott, Elizabeth Poole, and Teemu Taira showed that the number of articles in the *Guardian* mentioning "atheism", "secularism", "religion", and "faith" increased between 2005 and 2009 from 57 to 152, 76 to 113, 1,796 to 2,327, and 2,981 to 3,975 respectively. Nor was this increase limited to the *Guardian*, or indeed to recent years. Between 1982 and 2008-2009, they measured, "there was a rise in the number of references [to religion] overall, though with arguably less in-depth treatment, and an increase in media coverage of both religious diversity and the secular sacred."[34]

Some of this increase was about Christianity (though the uplift on account of Pope Francis lay some way ahead) but the majority of it was down to the clerical sex abuse scandal, the on-going tensions within the Anglican communion, the emergence of political Islam, and the explosion of aggressive atheism.

*Theos was founded a month after The God Delusion was published, and it is fair to say that the waters into which we were launched were fairly choppy.*

The growth of Islam was already clear in 2006. The increase in the size of the UK Muslim population has been noted, but this, of course, is merely the stage for the more dramatic public concerns about the number of British Muslims and their alleged threat to British culture and security. Thus, according to a YouGov poll conducted for the *Huffington Post* on the tenth anniversary of the 7/7 bombings, a majority of people (56%) considered Islam (as distinct from Islamic fundamentalist groups) to pose a threat to Western liberal democracy (a proportion that had increased since 9/11 and 7/7). In addition to this, the survey reported that 15% agreed that "a large proportion of British Muslims feel no sense of loyalty to this country and are prepared to condone or even carry out acts of terrorism" (again an increase since 7/7), while only a fifth said that practically all British Muslims are "peaceful and law-abiding and deplore terror attacks carried out in the name of Islam."[35] The point of quoting these data (others might have been cited[36]) is not to claim that the figures describing the British public's attitude to Muslims are an accurate representation of Muslims' attitude to the British public: some claim they are, some claim they are nothing more than Islamophobia, and have no more grounding in reality than the public view of the number of Muslims in Britain. It is rather to say that domestic and international politics will ensure that the issue of *religion* in British public life, albeit driven by one particular incarnation of one particular religion, will remain centre stage for the foreseeable future.

The growth of the second trend – aggressive atheism – was not so evident in 2006. Although Sam Harris' book *The End of Faith* was published in 2004, the movement was yet to gather steam and the term 'New Atheism' was itself only coined in 2006.[37] By some quirk of divine humour, Theos was founded a month after *The God Delusion* was published, and it is fair to say that the waters into which we were launched were fairly choppy. For some years it seemed the height of wit to declare that religious people worshipped Bronze Age sky pixies, believed the universe was manufactured in six days, and would unleash a murderous crusade or Inquisition given half the chance. Some still feel it is. The year 2006 also saw the launch of Twitter which became a useful soapbox for such views, even if some of the more prominent atheists subsequently proved themselves a little injudicious in their choice of tweets. The movement, and the reactions it spawned, was another example of religion elbowing its way centre stage, perhaps most famously when, in 2008, a group of atheists crowd-funded a bus-advert which told people "There's probably no God. Now stop worrying and enjoy your life", a campaign to which Theos contributed.[38]

Although the clerical sex abuse scandal, the Anglican Communion, Islam (and the rise of Islamophobic violence), and atheism have dominated the religion media headlines over the last decade, another UK contextual religious story is worth mentioning, namely the persistent presence (and apparent growth[39]) of anti-Semitism. On the one hand, Britain has one of the lowest rates of anti-Semitism in the world, according to Anti-Defamation League's (ADL) *Global 100: An Index of Anti-Semitism*, published in May 2014.[40] On the other, research from the Campaign Against Antisemitism (CAA) found that a sizeable minority of Britons agreed with two or more "stereotypical statements deemed by the CAA to be anti-Semitic in nature". "Whilst antisemitism in Britain is not yet at the levels seen in most of Europe," the CSS warned, "the results of our survey should be a wakeup call. Britain is at a tipping point."[41]

One final contextual religious narrative is also worth noting, if only in passing, namely the global growth in religion. The last decade saw greater evidence (although hard data remain elusive) for the significant growth of Christianity in the world's fastest growing major economy, China. China appears more typical, at least in terms of the future of the world, than the UK. According to a 2015 Pew Forum study into *The Future of World Religions*, over the next four decades Christianity will remain the world's largest religious group, although the number of Muslims will come nearly to equal the number of Christians,[42] and will account for a tenth of Europe's population, while "atheists, agnostics and other people who do not affiliate with any religion will make up a declining share of the world's total population."[43]

Such long-term, large-scale forecasts are always open to challenge, being based on certain semi-predictable trends – such as demography and conversion rates – and being by definition blind to most others (politics, events, revolutions, shifts in migration patterns, etc.). The combination of migration, the visit of Pope Benedict, the election of Pope Francis, and the full revelations of clerical sex abuse scandals all shaping the public presence of the Catholic Church in Britain, and all wholly unpredictable four decades ago, suggest that we should treat such long-range forecasts with some reservations. Moreover, even were such global religious forecasts to be more certain, quite how they might affect the course of *Christianity* in the UK is open to even greater doubt. Nevertheless, one can at least say with some confidence that whatever the future holds for Christianity in the UK, religion will remain an issue of interest and importance for the human species.

## conclusion

One broader trend relating to the well-documented emergence of the 'spiritual but not religious' category has been omitted from this opening chapter and will be dealt with in the next, for reasons that should become obvious. In the meantime, the objective of this chapter bears repeating by way of a conclusion. The intention has not been to depress those concerned about the future of Christianity in the UK, although some of the statistics are depressing. Rather, it has been to offer an honest perspective, both fine-detail and wide-angle on that future.

That perspective shows a main plot of the rapid decline of Christian nominalism and the slower decline of Christian commitment. It shows a number of sub-plots which suggest that the picture is not entirely straightforward or predictable. The very fact that the David Voas research showed that the key correlation for Church of England congregational growth is simply the serious desire to grow – "What's needed to make churches grow is that they should want to, and that the congregation should take the task seriously"[44] – should serve as an animating counterbalance to some of the more sobering statistics outlined. And it shows a range of contextual stories that illustrate that, whatever the future holds for Christianity in the UK, the broader questions of religion and faith are liable to remain somewhere near the centre of the radar for many years to come.

The consequence is that Christianity is now one religion in a variegated and confusing landscape. Christianity has contributed an incomparable amount to the formation of British, European, and Western civilisation (a theme of several Theos publications[45]) – indeed it has arguably been the foundation for the aforementioned civilisation – and for that reason at least, merits a distinct and (to adopt a word used by its critics) 'privileged' position at the heart of our national culture. That recognised, if the trends highlighted above point to anything, it is that the common Christian culture into which virtually every English, Scottish, Welsh and Northern/Irish person has been born for the last millennium is passing, to be replaced by a confusing plural patchwork, haunted by strong Christian associations. For a nation that has been comparably sure of its foundations for a very long time this leads us to unchartered and disconcerting territory.

# chapter 1 – references

1  The precise figures are, of course, highly tentative, as uncertainties abound as to the level and spread of church attendance at any one time, and even to the total UK population size. Indeed, it is astonishing quite how hard it is to get accurate and reliable data on a topic, like church attendance, about which everyone seems to know what is going on. I am very grateful to David Voas, Peter Brierley, Grace Davie, and David Goodhew for their feedback on these figures and how they have been calculated. For those interested in the details, this figure is calculated from the following sources:

According to British Religion in Numbers (BRIN), Religious affiliation and church attendance in Britain, 1983-2008, (http://www.brin.ac.uk/figures/#ChurchesandChurchgoers) 15.3% of the population of Britain said they attended church once a month or more in 2006. With a UK population of approximately 60 million people in 2006, that translates into an approximate *monthly* attendance of 9.2 million people. It is not clear how this figure would translate into a reliable weekly figure, but one would be inclined to halve it in doing so. It is, incidentally, quite possible that reported church attendance is also exaggerated church attendance, as it is in the US, although it is doubtful whether British respondents feel any pressure to say they go to church when they don't, and there is plenty of anecdotal evidence of pressures other way (cf. the amusing opening pages to Francis Spufford's *Apologetic* (Faber, 2015)).

According to a 2007 Tearfund study into churchgoing in the UK (http://news.bbc.co.uk/1/shared/bsp/hi/pdfs/03_04_07_tearfundchurch.pdf), 7.6 million UK adults (15%) attend at least monthly and 4.9 million (10% of UK adults) attend at least weekly. The Tearfund study adds that, including fringe and occasional churchgoers would bring the figure up by a further 5 million. The issue of fringe and occasional churchgoers is an important one, to which we will return in the text, although this seems to be an excessive figure.

The 2005 English Church Census reported that 6.3% of the population attended church on Census Sunday (8 May 2005), translating into 3,166,200 people (adults and children). This figure pertains to England and not to the UK. The population of England was approximately 51 million in 2006, that of Scotland about 5 million, Wales about 3 million, and Northern Ireland about 1.7 million. Assuming roughly a similar church attendance rates in Wales and Scotland to that of England, and a weekly church attendance rate of 45% for the Northern Ireland (as recorded by the 2007 Tearfund survey, although an improbably high figure), this adds respectively 315,000, 189,000, and 765,000 churchgoers, bringing the total to 4.48 million.

The final figure chosen is much closer to the English census figure for 2005 than the others, partly because of the constituent data from different denominations (see below) and partly because the Tearfund and BRIN surveys are based on respondent recall and therefore liable to some overclaim.

2  According to BSA 26 (2009/10) 10% of people in Great Britain said they attended a religious service "at least weekly". (A further 8% said they attended at least monthly.) That figure drops to about 8% for attending a church service weekly. Of the BSA figure, 20% were Anglican, 24% Catholic, and 37% other Christian denomination. These figures translate to weekly attendance rates of 1.25 million, 1.48 million, and 2.35 million for the three traditions respectively. This

seems slightly on the high side (about 300,000 higher than the figure quoted above). In particular, given that the Latin Mass Society measures Mass attendance in 2005 as 0.94 million (http://faithsurvey.co.uk/catholics-england-and-wales.html) the Catholic figure seems particularly high. If we can at least assume that the percentages within the BSA data are about right they would translate to roughly 1.15, 1.35, and 2.15 million Anglicans, Catholics and other Christians respectively. This first figure broadly concurs with those of the Church of England itself for 2006, c. 1.1 million. See *Statistics for Mission 2014*, Research and Statistics Department Archbishops' Council.

3    For Anglican figures see *Statistics for Mission 2014*, Research and Statistics Department Archbishops' Council. For the Catholic figure: according to the Latin Mass Society, 0.89 million Catholics attended weekly Mass in 2010 (http://faithsurvey.co.uk/catholics-england-and-wales. html). According to the Pastoral Research Trust Centre, the figure was 0.85 million in 2012 (http://www.prct.org.uk/downloads/20-population-statistics-2011-2012-6th-edition/file). The other figure is based on the widely recognised fact that levels of immigration have increased churchgoing in the UK, especially in the non-mainline denominations, and will have offset any decrease similar to that experienced among Anglicans and Catholics.

Peter Brierley, in personal correspondence, calculated a figure of 4.15 million in 2015 based on the actual English attendance of English membership (as given in UK Church Statistics No 2) and applied to the other three nations.

It should be noted that these figures, like the ones for 2006, may be at the lower end of the spectrum. For example, according to BSA2014, 18% of Anglicans, 40% of Catholics, and 34% of Other Christians attend church once a month or more often. Given that BSA 2014 gives the respective proportions of these groups in Britain as 18%, 8% and 17%, this works out as nearly 7.5 million church attendees (2 million Anglicans, 2 million Catholics, 3.5 million other) once a month or more, which seems improbably high even given the monthly as opposed to weekly timeframe.

It is also worth noting that it is possible that there is substantial undercounting of 'new churches', particularly BME and immigrant churches. For more on why this might be so see *Being Built Together: A Story of New Black Majority Churches in the London Borough of Southwark* (http://www.roehampton.ac.uk/uploadedFiles/Page_Content/Courses/Humanities/Being_ Built_Together/Being%20Built%20Together(SB)%203-7-13.pdf) and *New Churches in the North East* (http://community.dur.ac.uk/churchgrowth.research/research/new-churches-in-the-north-east).

Overall, as the amount of approximation in these various figures shows, this remains a subject very much more written about than genuinely understood.

4    It is worth noting that this is not a view shared by all commentators. See for example Bob Jackson, whose 2015 book *What Makes Churches Grow? Vision and Practice in Effective Mission* (London: Church House Publishing, 2015) says "the balance of the evidence suggests that the Church of England has probably stopped shrinking numerically and, on some measures, may even be growing overall" (p. xiv).

5    My own experience, rooted in conducting qualitative research into religious identity and belief over ten years ago, is that as long as one doesn't confuse affiliation with belief, behaviour or

attendance, it *can* mean a great deal. I interviewed a series of groups that, broadly speaking, believed the same thing (i.e. they weren't Christian believers though some believed in God and some didn't) and did the same thing (i.e. not attend church) but affiliated in different ways (some were 2001 census 'Christians', some were 'Nones'). The differences in attitude between the groups could be severe.

6   It is worth recognising that the census records higher levels of Christian affiliation than do everyday polls, and there is an animated debate over which is the better reflection of reality. It is also worth noting that this is the only optional question on the Census, which is one of the reasons why the figures do not add up to 100% here.

7   This total of 47% underlines the fact that the census tends to return disproportionately high figures; critics say it 'inflates' them.

8   http://www.theguardian.com/commentisfree/2016/jan/20/no-religion-britons-atheism-christianity

9   Cf. Andrew Brown's comment, "[Nominal Anglicans] are now being replaced by children and grandchildren who are unfervent nonbelievers." http://www.theguardian.com/commentisfree/2016/jan/20/no-religion-britons-atheism-christianity

10   See, Gareth Longden, 'A Profile of the Members of the British Humanist Association' [BHA], *Science, Religion & Culture*, Vol. 2, No. 3, June 2015, pp. 86-95; http://smithandfranklin.com/journal-details/Science-Religion-and-Culture/9/archive/2015/June

11   See David Voas and Siobhan McAndrew, 'Three Puzzles of Non-religion in Britain', *Journal of Contemporary Religion*, 27 (1): 29-48. http://dx.doi.org/10.1080/13537903.2012.642725

12   http://www.theosthinktank.co.uk/comment/2007/12/08/only-1-in-8-people-know-the-christmas-story-well

13   http://www.biblesociety.org.uk/press/uploads/final-copy-of-Pass-it-On-research-report_02070706.pdf

14   Clive Field, 'Is the Bible Becoming a Closed Book? British Opinion Poll Evidence', *Journal of Contemporary Religion*, 2014, Vol. 29, No. 3, 503–528; http://www.tandfonline.com/doi/pdf/10.1080/13537903.2014.945735 Interestingly, the article also concluded that people do not necessarily view the diminished status of the Bible as incompatible with, or undermining, the Christian faith, which indicates a shift within, as well as beyond, British Christianity itself.

15   http://www.brentcross.co.uk/events/nativity-naivety

16   http://www.bbc.co.uk/news/uk-12075931

17   https://www.ipsos-mori.com/researchpublications/researcharchive/3188/Perceptions-are-not-reality-the-top-10-we-get-wrong.aspx

18   http://www.ons.gov.uk/ons/rel/census/2011-census/detailed-characteristics-for-local-authorities-in-england-and-wales/sty-religion.html

19   http://www.churchgrowthresearch.org.uk/statistics_age_profile

20    Longden, 'A Profile of the Members of the British Humanist Association', http://smithandfranklin. com/journal-details/Science-Religion-and-Culture/9/archive/2015/June.  Moreover, 37% were already retired in 2014, compared with only 14% in 1964.

21    NatCen Social Research, 'Religion: Losing faith?' *British Social Attitudes* 28: 12.  http://www.bsa. natcen.ac.uk/media/38958/bsa28_12religion.pdf

22    Far more interesting would be data on the retention rates among attending groups, but I am not aware of this.

23    David Goodhew, 'Church Growth in Britain: A Response to Steve Bruce', *Journal of Religion in Europe 6* (2013) 297–315, p. 302.

24    Moreover, Goodhew has noted that other, more detailed studies of London churches indicate that this may be an undercount. See *Being Built Together: a Story of New Black Majority Churches in the London Borough of Southwark*, (University of Roehampton, 2013); Colin Marchant, 'The Growth of the Churches in Newham, 1980 to 2015', in D. Goodhew and A. Cooper (eds.), *No Secular City: Church Growth and Decline in London, 1980 to the Present*, (OUP, forthcoming).

25    See: Brierley, *UK Church Statistics 2*: 2010-20; D. Voas, 'Church of England Growth and Decline since 1980', in D. Goodhew, *Growth and Decline in the Anglican Communion, 1980 to the Present Day*, (Ashgate, 2016), p. 15; cf. also chapters by C. Marsh and K. Roxburgh in Goodhew (ed.) *Church Growth in Britain*, (Ashgate/ Routledge, 2012) and *New Churches in the North East* (Durham University, 2015).

26    http://www.pewforum.org/2012/03/08/religious-migration-overview-of-migrants-origins-and-destinations/

27    Goodhew, 'Church Growth', (2013) p. 306.

28    Pentecostal membership, for example, was 433,000 in 2012, and 'New' churches had an attendance figure of 210,000 in the UK in 2012. Brierley, *UK Church Statistics* 2: 2010-20.

29    http://www.economist.com/news/britain/21685473-parts-established-church-are-learning-their-immigrant-brethren-resurrection

30    http://www.churchgrowthresearch.org.uk/report See also David Voas and Laura Watt, *The Church Growth Research Programme Report on Strands 1 and 2: Numerical change in church attendance: National, local and individual factors*, September 2014 and http://www. churchgrowthresearch.org.uk/UserFiles/File/Presentations/CGRP_Voas.pdf cf also Church of England's *From Evidence to Action* (http://www.fromevidencetoaction.org.uk/) but also note Revd Dr Mark Hart's critical analysis of this 'From Delusion to Reality: An Evaluation of *From Anecdote to Evidence*', which highlights what he sees as a number of major weaknesses in the report. http://revmarkhart.blogspot.co.uk/2015/04/from-delusion-to-reality.html

31    http://www.baptist.org.uk/Articles/450911/Baptist_Union_Council.aspx It is worth noting that these figures were somewhat different from the perceived reality among Baptist Union churches which reported 36% of churches growing, 49% constant and 13% declining.

32    http://www.churchgrowthresearch.org.uk/UserFiles/File/Reports/Strand_3a_Cathedrals_Greater_Churches_draft_final_report_07_11_13.pdf

33    https://www.theguardian.com/world/2005/dec/05/religion.commentanddebate

34   Knott, K., Poole, E., Taira, T., *Media Portrayals of Religion and the Secular Sacred: Representation and Change* (Ashgate, 2013), chapters 4 and 5.

35   http://www.huffingtonpost.co.uk/2015/07/03/77-bombings-muslims-islam-britain-poll_n_7694452.html

36   For example, from British Future: http://survation.com/wp-content/uploads/2015/06/British-Future-7-7-Poll-GB-Tables.pdf; Centre for Fascist, Anti-Fascist and Post-Fascist Studies: http://www.tees.ac.uk/docs/DocRepo/Research/Tell_Mama3.pdf )

37   See Thomas Zenk, 'New Atheism', in Stephen Bullivant and Michael Ruse (eds.), *Oxford Handbook of Atheism* (Oxford: OUP, 2013), pp. 249-50. Also, Gary Wolf, 'The Church of the Non-Believers,' *Wired*, Issue 14.11, November 2006.

38   Not, it should be reasonably obvious, because we agreed with the message, let alone admired its profundity, but because as an attempt to get people thinking about God we felt it was to be encouraged.

39   According to a *Sunday Times* poll, 13% considered that, as regards other people, there was more prejudice against Jews than ten years ago. See https://d25d2506sfb94s.cloudfront.net/cumulus_uploads/document/wt26kxdn72/YG-Archive-Pol-Sunday-Times-results-160115.pdf

40   http://global100.adl.org/ For a summary of the findings see http://www.brin.ac.uk/2014/adl-index-of-anti-semitism/

41   The statements were, in order of 'popularity', "Jews chase money more than other British people" (25%), "Jews' loyalty to Israel makes them less loyal to Britain than other British people" (20%), "Jews think they are better than other people" (17%), "Jews have too much influence in the media" (17%), "Jews talk about the Holocaust too much in order to get sympathy" (13%), "In business Jews are not as honest as most people" (11%), and "I would be unhappy if a family member married a Jew" (10%). See https://d25d2506sfb94s.cloudfront.net/cumulus_uploads/document/jqf80l3ea6/CampaignAgainstAntisemitismResults_MergedFile_W.pdf . See also YouGov research conducted for *The Sunday Times* in January 2015, among 1,647 respondents, which found that "hard-core" prejudice against Jews "may not exceed 10% of the population". https://d25d2506sfb94s.cloudfront.net/cumulus_uploads/document/wt26kxdn72/YG-Archive-Pol-Sunday-Times-results-160115.pdf

42   With four out of every 10 Christians in the world living in sub-Saharan Africa.

43   http://www.pewforum.org/2015/04/02/religious-projections-2010-2050/

44   http://www.theguardian.com/commentisfree/andrewbrown/2014/jan/18/church-growth-theology-evangelical-lesson-liberals Or in the words of the report's authors, "There are no strong connections between growth and worship style, theological tradition, and so on. What seems crucial is that congregations are constantly engaged in reflection: churches cannot soar on autopilot. Growth is a product of good leadership (lay and ordained) working with a willing set of churchgoers in a favourable environment."

45   See Nick Spencer, *Freedom and Order: History, Politics and the English Bible* (Hodder and Stoughton, 2012), and *The Evolution of the West: Christianity and the Origin of our Values* (SPCK, 2016). See also Larry Siedentop, *Inventing the Individual: The Origins of Western Liberalism* (Allen Lane, 2014).

# comfortable unbelief?

In his 2007 intellectual blockbuster, *A Secular Age*, Canadian philosopher Charles Taylor charts the story of how, in 1500, it was "virtually impossible not to believe in God", whereas 500 years later "faith, even for the staunchest believer, is one human possibility among others."[1]

It is a complex and absorbing tale, a deliberate counter-story to the received wisdom of what he calls the 'subtraction narrative', in which secularisation has been a slow process of divesting ourselves of religious beliefs and practices until we find our true, naked, secular selves underneath. This Taylor, points out, is a woefully inadequate story and he spends many of his 800 pages explaining not only how we acquired secular selves that could conceive of living satisfactorily within a wholly 'immanent frame', but then explaining what we did when we got them.

> *The ancient human fascination with the divine or transcendent did not come to an end when we arrived at an 'immanent frame'.*

The ancient human fascination with the divine or transcendent did not come to an end when we arrived at an 'immanent frame', but, instead, found its expression in what Taylor calls the nova effect, "an ever-widening variety of moral/spiritual options". This in turn spawned a supernova effect in which "the fractured culture of the nova…becomes generalised to whole societies."[2] Ultimately, he writes towards the end of the book:

> Our world is ideologically fragmented, and the range of positions are growing… There are strong incentives to remain within the bounds of the human domain, or at least not to bother exploring beyond it. The level of understanding of some of the great languages of transcendence is declining… The individual pursuit of happiness as defined by consumer culture still absorbs much of our time and energy… All this is true, and yet the sense that there is something more presses in. Great numbers of people feel it: in moments of reflection about their life; in moments of relaxation in nature; in moments of bereavement and loss… *Our age is very far from settling into a comfortable unbelief.*[3]

This is a point of great importance for the future of Christianity in the UK (and beyond). Were it to be the case that the decline of Christian belief and commitment and what Taylor calls the 'social imaginary' that goes with it had left the modern world completely indifferent to questions of belief and entirely comfortable with life today – as many predicted it would – the future for Christianity would look bleak indeed. How do you talk a language of the spirit to a people for whom it is literally incomprehensible or meaningless?

It is important to recognise at this juncture that there is a stratum within society, especially concentrated in Western European and coastal American society, which *is* largely indifferent to belief and comfortable with life. Indeed, Taylor himself proceeds to recognise that "many individuals do [settle into comfortable unbelief], and more still seem to on the outside."[4] No essay on the future of Christianity should ignore this group or the wider fact that in any age, especially a 'secular age', there will be people who simply would not get it.

What is equally important to recognise, however, is that for all that such people are disproportionately significant in their shaping of the West's self-understanding, they are neither ubiquitous nor representative of the wider public.[5] Just because there is an educated and highly articulate and influential stratum in society for whom matters spiritual are incomprehensible or irrelevant, that doesn't mean that they speak for everyone. As Taylor puts it, "the unrest continues to surface."

This chapter begins by looking at that continually-surfacing 'unrest'. Any future for Christianity in 21st century Britain needs to take account not only of the state of Christianity (as we did in chapter one) but also of the state of Britain. Understanding our broader spiritual landscape is critical to this and comprises the first part of this chapter.

The second part then looks at another landscape – or, perhaps, another aspect of the same broader landscape – in which 21st century Christianity operates. For all that Christianity is about 'life after death', in popular parlance, it is at least as much about life before it.[6] So it is that to think creatively about the future of Christianity involves not only understanding what people believe about 'life eternal' but how they live 'life temporal'. Section two thus draws on a wide range of data (mostly confined to footnotes for the sake of readability) to analyse how we live today. As with chapter one, this can make for sobering reading and, without getting any more apocalyptic than we did there, it is clear that, for all our wealth and comparative luxury, we have reason to be concerned about many aspects of contemporary life.

# life eternal

Belief in the traditional Christian creeds has fallen over recent decades. According to a 2015 YouGov poll, 30% of people believed that Jesus was the son of God, 37% that he was a "real historical figure but not the Son of God", and 14% that he did not exist. Similarly, 29% of people said they believed he was resurrected, compared with 50% who said he did not come back to life after the crucifixion. Similar stories could be told about the levels and trends of belief in the Christmas story,[7] which have been declining over recent decades.[8] In much the same way, belief in God has also fallen over recent years. According to the same YouGov poll, 32% of adults in Britain believe in God and a further 20% in "a spiritual higher power", compared to 33% who said they don't believe in God.[9]

For all that such studies reveal a mixed public opinion, neither homogenously believing nor atheistic, it is nonetheless true that figures for belief in God have been on the same trajectory as those for affiliation and attendance over recent years. Thus, while the relevant surveys (of belief in God or a life force) collated by the British Religion in Numbers resource average out at 67% of people believing in the 1990s, those in the 2000s average out at 57%.[10] It appears that belief in God has been declining, albeit not at the rate of nominal Christian affiliation.

There is, however, more nuance to this narrative than the headline graph reveals, and it is important to recognise that not believing in God does not mean *not* retaining any spiritual beliefs or settling into Charles Taylor's "comfortable unbelief". While there may have been a rejection of organised religious belief in the later 20th century and early 21st, there has also been a turning towards looser, more amorphous, personalised, and often consumerised 'spiritual' beliefs (and practices). According to a 2016 YouGov study, over a fifth of the general public (and sometimes rather more) claimed to believe in an afterlife, fate, heaven, an everlasting soul, angels, ghosts, telepathy, karma, and reincarnation.[11]

Such data have been confirmed by various studies Theos has commissioned over the last ten years. In one 2012 study over a third (35%) of 'Nevers' (i.e. people who answered 'never' in response to the question "How often do you participate in a religious service as a worshipper?") expressed a belief in God or a Higher Power.[12] Around a third of people who belong to no-religion, over a quarter of 'Nevers', and 15% of atheists said that they believed in life after death. One in five 'Nevers' said they believed in angels. Just over a quarter of the general population said they believed in reincarnation, whilst just over a fifth of 'Nevers' agreed, and one in seven atheists. More than two in five 'Nevers' believed in a human soul, as did almost a quarter of atheists. Around one in six people who said they had 'no religion' considered themselves to be very or moderately spiritual. A quarter of the non-religious believed in heaven and 15% in hell. A fifth of non-religious people believed in the supernatural powers of deceased ancestors, compared to 23% of the total sample. While it is difficult to discern any clear or detailed picture from this blizzard of statistics, the data do reveal an extensive hinterland of spiritual beliefs and, conversely, a very low proportion of people (9%) who were consistent, thorough and coherent in their 'unbelief'.[13]

Such findings were confirmed by subsequent Theos research[14] and by other studies. According to a 2015 YouGov study, 68% of people said that death scared them "a lot" or "a little", while 36% said they definitely or probably believed in an afterlife.[15] According to another, a fifth of Britons believe that star signs "can tell you something about yourself or another person".[16] According to research by OnePoll conducted in 2014, although 76% of people in the UK do not regard themselves as "religious" (a seemingly dirty word in today's lexicon), over a third of these believe in God, over a quarter "ever attend religious services", nearly a third want a religious funeral, over two in five pray, and, remarkably, 6% say grace at mealtimes.[17] Further studies confirm the picture.[18]

Such data have been analysed in various ways, such as the emergence of a 'fuzzy faith', or of personalised, or individualised, or consumerised spirituality, or even of an apophatic faith, in which the unknown is given priority. However it is interpreted, the result is to confirm with various pinpricks of empirical evidence Taylor's thesis about the supernova effect. There are certainly trends downwards in orthodox and institutionalised and traditional Christian beliefs, but it would be a mistake to take this as a smooth and predictable journey towards "comfortable unbelief". Instead there are "cross-pressures" and cross-fertilisations, different and unpredictable trajectories, a mix of social imaginaries, tensions, and dilemmas which result in a variegated and complex plural landscape in which neither belief nor unbelief 'wins out'.

A neat, if very specific, illustration of this can be glimpsed in David Voas' paper *The mysteries of religion and the lifecourse* which drew on the 1970 British Cohort Study, which, in its 2012 wave, asked questions on belief in God and life after death as well as religious affiliation and practice, in such a way as to allow us to get a snap shot of the complexity of religiosity among one particular cohort.[19] The paper points out that gender differences in religious belief are very substantial[20] (an important point that is beyond the scope of this essay), and puts forward a seven-fold religious 'typology' to cover the various different combinations and permutations generated by the data of this cohort alone. This comprises

- the "non-religious", who do not have a religion and believe in neither God nor life after death, and comprise 28% of the cohort;

- the "nominally religious", who identify with a religion, but believe in neither God nor life after death, and comprise 7% of the cohort;

- the "unorthodox non-religious", who do not have a religion or attend services, but believe in God or life after death, but not both. These comprise 21% of the cohort;

- the "unorthodox religious", who have a religion and attend services at least occasionally, believe in God but not life after death (or in a few cases, vice versa). These comprise 5% of the cohort;

- the "non-identifying believers", who do not have a religion, but believe in God and life after death, and comprise about 10% of the cohort;

- the "non-practising religious", who have a religion and believe in God and life after death, but do not attend services. These comprise 14% of the cohort;

- the "actively religious" who have a religion and believe in God and life after death, and attend services, and comprise about 15% of the of the cohort.

This study draws on a certain limited number of questions pertaining to religious belief, affiliation and practice (i.e. not the full range of broader spiritual belief, affiliation and practices touched on above) and is based solely on those who were 42 years old in 2012. In other words, the true picture of spiritual complexity in the UK is liable to be even more complex than this, already detailed, segmentation.

> The overall picture we have is very clearly not one of a settled "comfortable unbelief" but a lively, fermenting, complex storm of spiritual ideas, practices and commitments.

However one interprets this complexity, the overall picture we have is very clearly not one of a settled "comfortable unbelief" but a lively, fermenting, complex storm of spiritual ideas, practices and commitments. This may not be a sea on which British Christians have much experience sailing, or one that they instinctively feel comfortable on, but it is the truest picture of belief in contemporary Britain that we have.

## life temporal

Twin dangers attend any analysis of life in contemporary Britain. The first is to believe the media headlines are typical of national life, a position that encourages the view that Britain is crawling with racists, paedophiles, ASBOs, bogus asylum seekers, and Islamic terrorists. To some extent that is precisely what we do. Thus, according to MORI, on average we think teenage pregnancy is 25 times higher than official estimates put it at; nearly a third of us (29%) think we spend more on Job Seekers Allowance than on pensions (in fact we spend around 15 times more on pensions); over a quarter (26%) of people think foreign aid is one of the top two or three items of government expenditure (it actually comprises around 1.1% of expenditure); and we think that 31% of the population are immigrants, when the official figure is 13%.[21] If one is going to look at the state of contemporary Britain, it is important to look at the hard data, in as far as it is available, rather than just public perception.[22]

This resolution, however, leads to the second danger, namely: which hard data? The temporal well-being of a country is a vast and complex subject, unlikely to be described fully by single trends or data lines. So it is that those hard data you deem of greatest descriptive significance invariably reflect your own priorities.

For example, there are many 'hard data' describing our material well-being, which show unequivocally that, 2008 crash and subsequent recession notwithstanding, Britain has been growing steadily richer and more materially comfortable for over 50 years now. Life is undoubtedly better than it ever was, if you judge better to mean richer and more comfortable.

In a more mixed vein, the hard data on subjective personal well-being[23] are ambiguous, the average adult rating of life satisfaction in the UK in 2013 being 6.8 out of 10, marginally higher than the OECD average of 6.6 out of 10, and placing the UK 18th of 36 OECD countries.[24] If subjective well-being – how I feel about my life – is the keystone, we are doing moderately well.

By contrast, hard data, such as the figures amassed by Thomas Piketty in his blockbuster *Capital in the 21st Century*, show that for all that we have grown wealthier, material inequality has also grown steadily and, seemingly, inexorably. Given that such inequality has been linked with a wide range of social ills – Richard Wilkinson and Kate Pickett's *The Spirit Level* connects inequality with poorer life expectancy, mental illness, violence, and illiteracy, among many other things – the hard data therefore tell a somewhat more sobering story about contemporary life.

The data of choice are indicative of the worldview one assumes, and even of what understanding of the human and the good one has, whether that is primarily grounded in material comfort, or social equality, or personal liberty, or whatever else. There is no view from nowhere.

An analysis of contemporary life grounded in a Christian worldview should pay heed to each of these factors but, I would argue, pay still greater attention to the quality of our relationships that comprise our common life. If "God is love"[25] and humans creatures made to reflect that love, it follows that the best litmus test of a society is the extent to which love is embodied and sustained in the relationships that make up society.

At first glance, the data here are encouraging. According to the Office for National Statistics,[26] two-thirds of people in the UK, in 2011/12, thought people in their neighbourhood could be trusted.[27] Around four in ten (41%) exchange favours with neighbours,[28] whilst nearly three-quarters felt people in their neighbourhood get along with each other[29] and the same proportion are willing to help each other.[30]

That recognised, if we scratch beyond the surface of these data, a more worrying picture emerges. One example of this is loneliness, which has become a topic of significant concern over recent years. While the proportion of people who say they have someone they could call on for support if they needed advice about a serious personal or family matter is high, at over 88%, this also means that more than one in ten people do not have such relationships.[31] **In 2015, there were 7.7 million people in UK households who were living alone.**[32] According to ONS data, around a tenth of people feel lonely most of the time.[33] Professor Keith Willett, the NHS's most senior acute care doctor, has warned that the consequences of loneliness "are increasing, unremitting demand on healthcare, which will ultimately cripple the NHS."[34] Thus the Local Government Association has claimed that loneliness is a "major public health issue", and the charity Age UK said that the issue "blights the lives" of over a million older people.[35]

Another area of concern is family breakdown. Although the number and rate of divorces has fallen over recent years, partly, it is assumed, on account of prior cohabitation, 42% of all marriages are still expected to end in divorce, more than half of them before their tenth anniversary.[36] If one adds to this the fact that cohabitation is less stable still,[37] it is clear that relationship breakdown is problematic. Around one in four children now grow up without a mother or, more usually, a father (of whom an estimated one million have no meaningful contact with their fathers), with single-parent households 2.5 times more likely to be in poverty than couple families.[38]

There are innumerable reasons for these relational problems. To identify that there is a problem is not to identify its source or cause. Relational breakdown is often the result of severe debt or financial vulnerability (for all the relative material wealth in the UK,[39] levels of income and capital inequality are returning to historic levels,[40] levels of in-work poverty are growing,[41] as is debt,[42] with nearly one in five households reporting a heavy financial debt burden, rising to one in three in the lowest income decile.[43] The Citizen's Advice Bureau claims that 21 million British citizens do not have a £500 cushion in case of a financial emergency[44]). It is sometimes as a result of alcohol and drug abuse.[45] There is no silver bullet here because there is no single source of relational problems. The point being made, however, is that there is a problem.

Moreover, and importantly, one does not have to adhere to a Christian worldview framed by 'right relationships' to recognise that this is so. The sheer rise and level in the use of antidepressants – around one in 11 British adults now take antidepressants, according to the British Journal of Psychiatry[46] – is worrying. Calculations of Adult Psychiatric Morbidity in England 2007 estimated that one in four people in England will experience a mental health problem in any given year.[47] According to the ONS, in 2009/10, more than one in ten adults (11%) in England were diagnosed with depression.[48] According to the Journal of Psychopharmacology, there were 8.2 million cases of anxiety in the UK in 2013, with women are almost twice as likely to be diagnosed with anxiety disorders as men.[49] Whatever the changes in attitudes to and stigmas around medicalisation, the level of personal metal illness, depression, and anxiety in the UK is not healthy. Whether one's entry point into this debate is through social trust, or personal relationships, or individual psychological health, there is room for concern.

Perhaps the most worrying thing in all this is the disproportionate way it is affecting children and young people in the UK today. However well or otherwise British adults may be doing in terms of self-reported well-being, research shows that British teenagers are among the least contented in western world.[50] A 2016 report by the World Health Organisation (WHO) into the health, well-being, social environment and health behaviour of 11-, 13- and 15-year-old boys and girls across 42 countries found that British teenagers felt pressured at school, and worried by health, appearance and weight issues.[51] Many other studies confirm and fill out these findings.[52] According to another study, on the mental health of children and young people in Great Britain, one in ten of those aged 5-16 had a clinically diagnosable mental health problem. According to ONS, there were one in eight children aged 10 to 15 who reported symptoms of mental ill-health in 2011 to 2012.[53] Perhaps not surprisingly, antidepressant use by children is alarmingly high: a widely-reported study published in the *European Journal of Neuropsychopharmacology* in 2016, showed that between 2005 and 2012 there was a 54% increase in the number of young people prescribed them in the UK.[54] To proceed further would be to labour the point: however one looks at it, children growing up in Britain are not getting the best deal.

## conclusion

There are two wrong ways of reading the data and implicit argument in this chapter, and one right way.

The first wrong one is to assume that contemporary Britain is a bad place to live, or that people there are, as a rule, miserable. It isn't and they aren't. It is perfectly possible to live a contented, secure and socially-engaged life in Britain today, and not to feel isolated, depressed, anxious, indebted or otherwise uneasy. By historic standards and by many contemporary ones, the UK today is very good place to live. What the data, in a wide range of areas, do show is that the general sense of relative well-being can easily disguise deeper problems, particularly those related to our relational (and attendant emotional and mental) health. Material comfort and broadly positive levels of self-reported well-being should not blind us to real and sometimes surprisingly widespread pain.

This leads to the second misunderstanding, namely that Christianity is some kind of magic wand that we simply have to wave across the land to solve all these problems. It isn't and it wouldn't. Anyone with a cursory knowledge of social history will know that, for all the herculean efforts made by campaigning Christians in the 19th century against drink, debt, ill-health, prostitution and squalor, Victorian Britain was still scarred by all of these. Christianity can, does and should speak into these social needs, but to imagine it simply solves problems of obesity or debt is to live in fantasy land. Faith doesn't work like that.

If these are the wrong ways of understanding the argument of this chapter, what is the right way? To answer this it is necessary to return to the framing concept of this chapter. Too often, the present and future of Christianity in the UK is treated in an unsatisfactorily isolated way, a belief system that is divorced from the lived context – eternal and temporal – in which it exists. Bringing that context into focus underlines how the UK has not settled into the kind of comfortable unbelief of which Charles Taylor writes.

Moreover, doing this also helps bring into focus what Christianity might have to offer 21st century Britain. Christianity as belief and Christianity as belonging within a congregation are both important, indeed essential, but while apologetics and invitation services will continue to play key roles in the future, it is the contention of this essay that the first point of engagement will be in what the following chapter calls 'social liturgy'.

# chapter 2 – references

1   Charles Taylor, *A Secular Age* (Harvard/ Belknap, 2007), p. 3.

2   Ibid. p. 299.

3   Ibid. p. 727; emphases added

4   Such 'individuals' have been described as WEIRD, an acronym of Western, Educated, Industrialised, Rich and Democratic, and have been well analysed by Jonathan Haidt in his book, *The Righteous Mind: Why Good People Are Divided by Politics and Religion*. For the WEIRD, he argues, religion – or more precisely, its constituent elements of a sense of sanctity and of authority – is simply a taste bud that they don't have. Their moral compass and outlook on the world is comprised of different tastes, albeit ones often shared by religious people (he specifies care/harm, fairness/cheating, and loyalty/betrayal). Authority and sanctity, however, crucial as they are to the religious worldview, are either absent or very faint for them, thereby turning 'faith' into an alien, incomprehensible and/or superfluous entity.

5   Demographically speaking, such voices of 'comfortable unbelief' are not even entirely typical of Europe, or the UK, let alone the US. As is widely recognised, unbelief is disproportionately male. Thus, according to a study of more than 9,000 British people in their forties, published by UCL Institute of Education (IOE), more than half (54%) of the men surveyed said they were atheists or agnostics, compared to only a third (34%) of the women. See David Voas, 'The mysteries of religion and the lifecourse' http://www.ioe.ac.uk/newsEvents/110639.html As innumerable people pointed out, the New Atheist phenomenon was a conspicuously male storm. Similarly, according to the Theos research *Faith of the Faithless* discussed below, not only is the proportion of people who are consistent and coherent in their unbelief relatively small but the "typical" non-religious person is socio-demographically more likely than the population in general to be male, younger, and white, as well as slightly better educated and better off.

6   In reality, of course, the two are not the opposing binaries that many think, and the New Testament talk of the 'kingdom of God' self-consciously straddles the divide, with feet firmly planted in both life today and life eternal.

7   See https://yougov.co.uk/news/2014/12/24/public-opinion-christmas-story/

8   See BRIN, Figures, 7.31: http://www.brin.ac.uk/figures/#ChangingBelief

9   https://yougov.co.uk/news/2015/02/12/third-british-adults-dont-believe-higher-power/

10  See BRIN, Figures, 7.23: http://www.brin.ac.uk/figures/#ChangingBelief

11  https://yougov.co.uk/news/2016/03/26/o-we-of-little-faith/

12  Nick Spencer & Holly Weldin, *Post-religious Britain?: The faith of the faithless* (Theos, 2012) This report drew on data from three sources: a 2012 ComRes/Theos study primarily exploring the public's attitude to English cathedrals; a 2008 ComRes/Theos Darwin study (primarily exploring the public's attitude to evolution and religious belief); and the 2008 wave of the British Social Attitudes survey.

13  Specifically, who don't believe in God, never attend a place of worship, call themselves non-religious, and don't believe life after death, the soul, angels, etc.

14    For example, *The Spirit of Things Unseen*, which found that over three-quarters of all adults (77%) and three fifths (61%) of non-religious people believe that "there are things in life that we simply cannot explain through science or any other means." It reported that a majority of people (59%) are believers in the existence of some kind of spiritual being, 30% believe in God "as a universal life force", 30% in spirits, 25% in angels, and 12% in "a higher spiritual being that can't be called God." Nearly two in five people believe in the existence of a soul (39%), 32% in life after death, 26% in heaven, 16% in reincarnation, 13% in hell, and 13% in the power of deceased ancestors. In total, over half the British public (54%) holds at least one of these spiritual beliefs, whereas by comparison, only 13% of adults – and only 25% of the non-religious – agree with the statement "humans are purely material beings with no spiritual element".

15    https://d25d2506sfb94s.cloudfront.net/cumulus_uploads/document/zcui1w66ie/Copy%20 of%20Opi_InternalResults_150817_Death_R_W_2.pdf

16    https://yougov.co.uk/news/2015/07/03/8-of-Britons-believe-horoscopes-predict-the-future/

17    Reported by British Religion in Numbers: http://www.brin.ac.uk/2014/religious-irreligious-and-other-news/

18    Thus British Religion in Numbers reports that 57% of people said that they believed in the existence of the soul in 2009 (70% having said so in another study the previous year); 53% of people said they believed in life after death in 2008; 46% of people said they believed in guardian angels in 2009; 27% of people said they believed in reincarnation in 2008; 22% of people said they believed in astrology in 2008.

19    David Voas, 'The mysteries of religion and the lifecourse', CLS working paper 2015/1 (London: Centre for Longitudinal Studies) http://www.cls.ioe.ac.uk/page.aspx?&sitesectionid=939&sit esectiontitle=Recent+working+papers This paper also includes the important caveat that "a close examination of the multiple waves of the BCS70 reveals a large amount of uncertainty in measurement, making it hard to detect whatever genuine change might have occurred." This is a salutary warning that should hang over all the trends discussed in this essay.

20    Specifically, according the Cohort Study 54% of men are atheists or agnostics compared with only 34% of women, whilst 35% of men believe in life after death compared with 60% of women.

21    More misconceptions are available here: https://www.ipsos-mori.com/researchpublications/ researcharchive/3188/Perceptions-are-not-reality-the-top-10-we-get-wrong.aspx It is worth noting that religion is far from immune to this problem. According to MORI, while we greatly overestimate the proportion of the population who are Muslims (24% vs. the reality of 5% in England and Wales), we rather underestimate the proportion of people who say that they are Christian (34% on average, compared, according to MORI, with the actual proportion of 59% in England and Wales).

22    That noted, the challenge is that even when gathering 'hard data' on this matter, one is reliant on opinion, as information on how neighbourly, or not, people are invariably comes from how neighbourly they think they are. This is an unavoidable challenge and means that however robust the data sets used, one always needs to proceed with care.

23  The Organisation for Economic Co-operation and Development (OECD) describe subjective (or personal) well-being as "reflect[ing] the notion that how people experience a set of circumstances is as important as the circumstances themselves, and that people are the best judges of how their own lives are going" (OECD, 2011).

24  https://www.gov.uk/government/uploads/system/uploads/attachment_data/file/277595/International_comparisons.pdf

25  1 John 4:8.

26  Specifically, The Office for National Statistics' 'Measuring national well-being: An analysis of social capital in the UK' http://www.ons.gov.uk/peoplepopulationandcommunity/wellbeing/articles/measuringnationalwellbeing/2015-01-29.

27  According to the Cabinet Office's Community Life Survey Statistical Bulletin, in 2013-14 70% of people felt that they belonged 'very' or 'fairly' strongly to their neighbourhood, although this represented a significant decrease from levels in 2005.

28  According to the Cabinet Office's Community Life Survey Statistical Bulletin, 44% of people 'definitely' or 'tended to' agree that they borrow things and exchange favours with their neighbours.

29  According to the Cabinet Office's Community Life Survey Statistical Bulletin, 85% of people were either 'very' or 'fairly' satisfied with their local area as a place to live and 85% of people thought that their community was cohesive.

30  According to the Cabinet Office's Community Life Survey Statistical Bulletin, in 2013-14, 60% of people agreed that people in their neighbourhood pull together to improve their neighbourhood. Further data confirm these findings. Nearly 1 in 5 people (19%) reported looking after or giving special help to someone sick, disabled or elderly either inside their household (8%) or outside their own household (11%). The same proportion (19%) said they had given unpaid help or worked as a volunteer in a local, national or international organisation or charity in the previous 12 months (again this is from 2012/13), and again about the same proportion (18%) had been involved in at least one social action project in their local area in the previous 12 months.

31  https://www.theguardian.com/news/datablog/2014/jun/18/uk-second-least-neighbourly-country-eu-after-germany

32  http://webarchive.nationalarchives.gov.uk/20160105160709/http://www.ons.gov.uk/ons/dcp171778_422175.pdf

33  Specifically: 11% of people in the UK reported feeling lonely all, most, or more than half of the time in 2011/12 (over previous two weeks).

34  http://www.theguardian.com/society/2016/feb/01/loneliness-forces-older-people-into-hospitals-and-strains-services-say-senior-doctors

35  http://www.telegraph.co.uk/news/health/news/12126606/Loneliness-is-a-major-public-health-issue-local-government-body-claims.html It should be noted that this isn't a problem limited to the elderly. According to one survey by the Church Urban Fund, this is a phenomenon that doesn't stop at age or class or neighbourhood boundaries – the CUF study found that

loneliness was as widespread a social problem in affluent, middle-class neighbourhoods as poorer ones – although the impression is that it particularly afflicts the elderly. https://gallery.mailchimp.com/50eac70851c7245ce1ce00c45/files/Church_in_Action_full_report_Feb_2015_Final.pdf

36   http://webarchive.nationalarchives.gov.uk/20160105160709/http://www.ons.gov.uk/ons/rel/vsob1/divorces-in-england-and-wales/2011/sty-what-percentage-of-marriages-end-in-divorce.html

37   For example, a study by the Institute for Fiscal Studies found that "cohabiting parents are more likely to split up than married ones" (http://www.ifs.org.uk/bns/bn107.pdf) and a report from Civitas stated: "Cohabiting relationships are fragile. They are always more likely to break up than marriages entered into at the same time, regardless of age or income. On average, cohabitations last less than two years before breaking up or converting to marriage. Less than four per cent of cohabitations last for ten years or more." (http://www.civitas.org.uk/content/files/cohabitation.pdf)

38   http://www.centreforsocialjustice.org.uk/UserStorage/pdf/Pdf%20reports/CSJ_Fractured_Families_Report_WEB_13.06.13.pdf

39   GDP per capita stands at around £28,000 http://webarchive.nationalarchives.gov.uk/20160105160709/http://www.ons.gov.uk/ons/rel/naa1-rd/united-kingdom-economic-accounts/q3-2015/index.html with the UK standing fourth across the EU in terms of standard of living. http://webarchive.nationalarchives.gov.uk/20160105160709/http://www.ons.gov.uk/ons/infographics/standard-of-living-in-the-european-union/index.html

40   See Thomas Piketty, *Capital in the 21st Century* (Harvard, 2014).

41   In the UK, 8% of people in employment were also in relative income poverty in 2013, equivalent to around 3 million people. http://webarchive.nationalarchives.gov.uk/20160105160709/http://www.ons.gov.uk/ons/dcp171776_395768.pdf

42   The total outstanding non-mortgage borrowing in the UK grew by nearly £20bn or 9% in 2014, to reach £239bn (the fastest rate of growth in a decade) PwC, *Precious Plastic: How Britons Fell Back in Love With Borrowing*, http://www.pwc.co.uk/industries/financial-services/insights/precious-plastic-2015.html

43   http://webarchive.nationalarchives.gov.uk/20160105160709/http://www.ons.gov.uk/ons/dcp171776_412308.pdf

44   Quoted by CEO of CAB at the Bank of England Open Forum 11 November 2015.

45   According to the Nuffield Trust, Accident and Emergency attendance rates likely to be due to alcohol poisoning more than doubled, from 72.7 per 100,000 population to 148.8 per 100,000 between 2008/09 and 2013/14. More generally, inpatient admissions specific to alcohol increased by two-thirds between 2005/06 and 2013/14. http://www.nuffieldtrust.org.uk/sites/files/nuffield/publication/alcohol-specific-activity_final-web.pdf Perhaps not surprisingly, according to *The Lancet*, mortality rates from liver disease have increased 400% since 1970, and in people younger than 65 years have risen by almost five-times. http://www.thelancet.com/commissions/crisis-of-liver-disease-in-the-UK When it comes to drug use, according to the

Home Office, around 1 in 12 (8.6%) of adults aged 16 to 59 had taken illegal drugs in 2014-15, rising to 1 in 5 (19.4%) of 16-24s. Altogether, over a third (34.7%) of adults had taken drugs at some point during their lifetime. https://www.gov.uk/government/uploads/system/uploads/attachment_data/file/462885/drug-misuse-1415.pdf

46   See Antidepressant use in 27 European countries: associations with sociodemographic, cultural and economic factors, Dan Lewer, Claire O'Reilly, Ramin Mojtabai, Sara Evans-Lacko, The British Journal of Psychiatry Sep 2015, 207 (3) 221-226; DOI: 10.1192/bjp.bp.114.156786 This compared unfavourably with other European countries (the UK level was the fourth highest proportion in the EU) and unfavourably with long-term historic data (with prescriptions dispensed for antidepressants increasing by 334% in England between 1991 and 2009) (Health, David Sweet, Social Trends 41, ONS, p. 4) and unfavourably with shorter-term data which showed that 12.5 million more antidepressants pills were prescribed in 2012 than in 2007. (http://www.nuffieldtrust.org.uk/publications/focus-antidepressant-prescribing) Some have argued that the context for this steep increase is a different attitude to taking of antidepressants, rather than different (i.e. worse) levels of depression. That is undoubtedly true but if true it is self-evidently only part of the truth.

47   See McManus S, Meltzer H, Brugha T, Bebbington P, Jenkins R (eds) (2009). Adult Psychiatric Morbidity in England 2007: results of a household survey. NHS Information Centre for Health and Social Care: http://www.hscic.gov.uk/pubs/psychiatricmorbidity07

48   Health, David Sweet, Social Trends 41, ONS, p. 4.

49   Fineberg, N., Haddad, P., Carpenter, L., Gannon, B., Sharpe, R., Young, A., Joyce, E., Rowe, J., Wellsted, D., Nutt, D. and Sahakian, B. (2013). The size, burden and cost of disorders of the brain in the UK. Journal of Psychopharmacology, 27(9), pp. 761-770.

50   http://www.theguardian.com/society/2016/mar/15/british-teenagers-among-least-satisfied-in-western-world

51   WHO, Growing up unequal: gender and socioeconomic differences in young people's health and well-being, http://www.euro.who.int/en/health-topics/Life-stages/child-and-adolescent-health/health-behaviour-in-school-aged-children-hbsc/growing-up-unequal-gender-and-socioeconomic-differences-in-young-peoples-health-and-well-being.-health-behaviour-in-school-aged-children-hbsc-study-international-report-from-the-20132014-survey

52   Green, H., McGinnity, A., Meltzer, H., Ford, T., Goodman, R. Mental Health of Children and Young People in Great Britain: 2004. Office for National Statistics (2005) http://www.hscic.gov.uk/catalogue/PUB06116/ment-heal-chil-youn-peop-gb-2004-rep2.pdf

53   https://www.ons.gov.uk/peoplepopulationandcommunity/wellbeing/articles/measuringnationalwellbeing/2015-10-20

54   http://www.bps.org.uk/news/concerns-over-rise-childrens-use-anti-depressant-drugs

# social liturgy

Were the data of decline, whether gentle or precipitous, outlined in the first chapter to be taken to their logical conclusion, we would expect to see not only fewer nominal and worshipping Christians, but also fewer *active* ones – fewer people serving, helping, pastoring, volunteering in their community. After all, heavily declining affiliation and slightly declining congregations leave a smaller pool from which such resources can be drawn.

It is, striking, therefore that, in as far as we are in a position to judge[1] this is not what we see. There may be fewer Christians but they are doing more. This is central to the argument of this chapter, and indeed this essay. Not only is the size of British Christianity changing, but so is its shape, the way in which it lives out its faith.

This chapter begins by looking at what the figures say about this 'Doing Good', before explaining why broader social and political trends suggest there is going to be an ever greater need for such action. It then moves on to one central and very important objection to this kind of action, in the process introducing the idea of social liturgy and offering a few examples of what it looks like. It concludes by arguing that the development of social liturgy also addresses a number of neuralgic issues that hover around the question of Christian presence in the public life of an increasingly plural society such as our own.

## the strange rise of Christian 'social action'

### the rise in provision

According to research from New Philanthropy Capital, there are nearly 50,000 faith-based charities in the UK, out of a total of nearly 188,000 registered charities. These charities receive 23%, or £16 billion, of the charity sector's income in England and Wales.[2]

Over the last decade, the number of 'faith-based' charities has grown, both in terms of the total and as a proportion of all charities, and there are around 15,000 more today than there were in 2006. Moreover, a higher proportion of faith-based charities (34%) were registered with the Charity Commission in the last ten years than non-faith ones (25%), the figure for Christian charities being 38%.[3] In other words, people of all religious faiths, and especially Christians, are disproportionately getting involved in social action in contemporary Britain. Such findings have been repeatedly confirmed by research conducted by Theos and other organisations over the last ten years.

> People of all religious faiths, and especially Christians, are disproportionately getting involved in social action in contemporary Britain.

Over 2013-14, Theos conducted research for the Church Urban Fund in which we set out to understand the impact of local churches in deprived communities in England.[4] This involved some detailed case studies and also included a ComRes quantitative study which asked a national representative sample of the population whether they, or an immediate family member, had accessed community (non-statutory) services in the last 12 months and whether they had been provided by churches or church groups. Around half (48%) of adults had accessed community services, with around half (51%) of these accessing services provided by churches or church groups.[5] Using ONS population figures for England, this equated to just over 10 million adults using church 'services', using the word explicitly to exclude the traditionally 'religious' services of Sunday, Christmas, Easter, and Harvest services, and baptisms, weddings, and funerals.

The services listed included foodbanks, community events (e.g. lunch clubs or cafes), healthy living activities (e.g. community nursing, exercise classes, healthy eating courses), relationship support, financial education and advice, access to computers/the internet, and providing opportunities for volunteering. The most frequently used community services were children and youth services, cultural events, and activities for older people, but churches also provided support for asylum seekers, for people with addictions, counselling and 'street pastoring'. In other words, the level of community activity among the churches was huge.

These CUF/ComRes findings have been amply repeated by other studies. Cinnamon Network emerged in 2010 as a response to growing recognition of the importance of faith-based organisations in the provision of social and community services. Five years later, it attempted to measure faith-based social action across the country, which it has published in its *Cinnamon Faith Action Audit National Report*.[6] The audit approached 4,440 local churches and other faith groups, about half of which responded saying that they were actively working to support their local community. Between them, these 2,110 groups (94% of which were church groups) had 9,177 paid staff, mobilised 139,600 volunteers and supported an estimated 3.5 million beneficiaries each year. The study calculated that the time alone given by churches and other faith groups surveyed was worth over £200 million, which nationally put the time given by churches and other faith groups into their communities through social action projects at over £3 billion a year.[7]

In the same year, Jubilee+, an organisation set up by Newfrontiers churches in the UK to encourage churches (of all denominations) in their community activity, published the results of the third biennial National Church and Social Action Survey.[8] This reported that somewhere between 1.1 and 1.4 million volunteers participated in church-based social action in the UK in 2014, the top ten initiatives being food distribution, parents and toddlers' groups, school assemblies/RE work, festivals/fun days, children's clubs,[9] caring for the elderly,[10] debt counselling, youth work,[11] café open to public, and marriage counselling/courses.[12] The particular value of this survey was that, being the third, it was able to give some indication of how such initiatives have changed over recent years.

The pattern was one of increase. The report found that churches had increased the average number of staff hours on social action by nearly a fifth in two years; increased the average number of volunteer hours on social action by nearly a sixth to 114.8 million hours per annum over the same two year period;[13] increased their spending on social action by nearly a seventh to approximately £393 million over the same two years;[14] and increased the average number of social action initiatives undertaken by a fifth from 7.4 to 8.9 during this period. Moreover, the study found that over half (58%) of churches planned to increase social initiatives in the next 12 months.[15]

Longitudinal trends need more than two or four years to be reliable, so these precise figures need to be treated with caution, in much the same way as the Cinnamon Audit's aggregated figures do, but this again constitutes a minor caveat. Jubilee+ showed what the Cinnamon Audit and the Theos/CUF/ComRes research implied: namely that the level of Christian social action is vast and growing.

## the rise in need

These various surveys repeatedly show how Christian social action is growing, how it is answering many of the real needs, such as those outlined in chapter two, and how it provides a powerful counter-narrative to those we heard in chapter one. More broadly, contextual trends suggest that this is not simply an anomaly of the moment but the direction of travel.

One of the major publications of recent years, Thomas Piketty's *Capital in the 21st Century* spends much time in analysing the golden age of state welfare, *Les Trente Glorieuses*, the 'Glorious Thirty' years after the war in which many Western countries experienced the happy combination of significant economic growth, enabling vastly expanded welfare provision, without exacerbating the (historically very low) levels of capital and income inequality with which they started. "When incomes are increasing five per cent a year," Piketty observed, "it is not too difficult to get people to agree to devote an increasing share of that growth to social spending."[16] Economists and politicians came to assume that this combination of economic growth, increased public spending and low and stable levels of inequality was the natural and inevitable direction of travel for modern societies. It wasn't.

All this began to change in the later 1970s, as a cash-strapped government placed spending limits on state welfare provision, the welfare state faced mounting criticism for its bureaucratic inefficiency (and, ironically, for patronising and infantilising welfare recipients: the same criticism that had been levelled so powerfully at the charitable sector), and the New Right reverted to the language of freedom, choice, independence, voluntary endeavour, and personal virtues, sometimes wrapping them up in colourful Victoriana.[17]

The extent to which this change in the weather was down to economic necessity or political opportunism remains much debated. Piketty himself sheds an interesting, and well-balanced, light on this. On the one hand, he credits the politics of Thatcherism and Reaganomics with much, including "the gradual privatization and transfer of public wealth into private hands",[18] and the determined financialisation of the global economy, allowing for the total amount of financial assets and liabilities held by various sectors (including households) to increase more rapidly (in some instances considerably more rapidly) than net wealth.

On the other, he is clear that while *Les Trente Glorieuses* did witness significant growth, longer term data show these were anomalous decades, years in which countries were effectively playing catch up after the destruction of the less than glorious thirty years that preceded them. (A similar logic of catch up is dictating the rapid growth of China and India in our own time.) When there is no catching up to be done, growth is naturally much lower, which means public spending becomes more difficult. "There is no historical example of a country at the world technological frontier whose growth in per capita output exceeded 1.5 percent over a lengthy period of time."[19] In other words, *Les Trente Glorieuses* would not have remained glorious even without Thatcher and Reagan.

Whether economic necessity or political opportunism or, rather, what combination of the two changed the weather, the opening years of the 21st century felt very different to the world of two generations earlier, and the need for voluntary social action was intense and growing.[20] Parties of every colour recognise the need for and encourage the engagement of faith-based voluntary activity in a wide range of contexts. This brings with it a number of tensions and challenges, some of which we touch on below, but these notwithstanding the overall message is clear: the need for and opportunity to demonstrate Christian love and commitment through concrete social action is greater today than it has been for generations.

## from social action to social liturgy

At this point, alarm bells may start ringing in many minds. Have we not been here before? Nice as it may be to be wanted, is the church really just a social service provider, a "compassionate NGO", in Pope Francis' words?[21] The short answer to these questions is 'Yes, we have' and 'No, it isn't'.

> There is a real and present danger in grounding the future of Doing God in the UK in the practice of Doing Good. If you are not careful, God becomes little more than Good or, even worse, feel-good.

The idea of the Christian gospel as social action is most often associated with the so-called Social Gospel, a movement that flourished among mainline Protestants around the turn of the 19th to 20th centuries in the US. Thoroughly committed to addressing the social and economic injustices that plagued rapidly industrialising America, the movement faded in the early decades of the 20th century and although there is no consensus as to why (the First World War, and the ensuing turmoil of the 20s and 30s, undermined its progressive optimism; Roosevelt's New Deal made some of it ambitions and activity redundant), there is also a sense that the movement began to detach its mission from its theological core, becoming, in effect, indistinguishable from any other social action. For wholly admirably if ultimately misguided reasons, love of neighbour eclipsed love of God.

There is a real and present danger in grounding the future of Doing God in the UK in the practice of Doing Good. If you are not careful, God becomes little more than Good or, even worse, feel-good. That is why this essay proposes a small but important conceptual shift, away from understanding the phenomenon as 'social action' to understanding it as 'social liturgy'.

Liturgy is popularly understood today to mean a form of corporate, public worship, saying the right things, with the right people, at the right time, in the right place, and very often wearing the right clothes. This, however, whilst being the popular understanding of the English word fails to do justice to the origins of the term.

'Liturgy' derives from the New Testament Greek word, *leitourgia*. Like all words, not least complex ones from historically distant cultures, *leitourgia* was used in different ways and can be understood to have meant different things (something that is further compounded by the fact that the word, although not uncommon in the ancient world, is used only six times in the New Testament).

In the first instance, the word was clearly used to mean a service that was obviously "religious" or sacrificial – a priestly or Levitical service that was conducted, more likely than not, within the Temple. Thus when Luke's gospel talks about priest named Zechariah, "who belonged to the priestly division of Abijah" and was husband of Elizabeth and father of John the Baptist, completing his "time of service in the Temple before returning home", it uses the word *leitourgia*.[22] Similarly, when the writer of the letter to the Hebrews speaks of the gifts and sacrifices offered by the high priest in the Temple, and then claims that the "ministry" of Jesus was superior to that of these high priests, he uses the word *leitourgia*.[23]

The word could also be used, however, in a less overtly "religious" sense to refer to the kind of charitable activity or gift or benefaction such as was central to the life of the earliest Christian communities. Thus, when Paul writes in his second letter to the church in Corinth praising them for their readiness to give and their enthusiasm for action, and commending their "service" in supplying the needs of the Lord's people, he uses *leitourgia*.[24] Similarly, when writing to the Philippians about his co-workers Timothy and Epaphroditus, he says of the latter that he risked his life "to make up for the help [or service] you yourselves could not give me", again using the word *leitourgia*.[25]

Sometimes, the word hovers between these two meanings, in such a way to as suggest the coherence of the term. Thus, a little earlier on in his letter to the Philippians, Paul writes how he is being "poured out like a drink offering on the sacrifice and *service* coming from your faith", thereby framing discussion of his own pastoral efforts in a sacrificial understanding.[26]

All language is somehow indeterminate and polysemous, resounding with echoes – some faint, some loud – of subtly different meanings. *Leitourgia* is certainly no different. What we can get from the term is that it captures the idea of generous, even selfless service, which could be directed at both the human and the divine other, and while the English word 'service' might itself be used to capture this dual-directed love, that word may fail to describe the God-directed nature of the action. Hence liturgy, obviously derived from *leitourgia*, and social liturgy, a self-consciously awkward term intended to capture the idea of charitable public action – working for and 'being with' the other – that is *also* deliberately God-conscious, or priestly.

I would suggest that this is precisely the kind of dual-focused mindset that needs to frame the kind of social action we are discussing; not simply social action that is devoid of any serious theological formation, nor Christian 'worship' that loves God and ignores one's neighbour, but social liturgy – the practice of public commitment to the other that is explicitly rooted in and shaped by love of God.

That love should serve to remind us that 'social action' or 'service' of this kind is not a matter of those who are OK dispensing largesse, however generous, to those who are not. It is a fundamental tenet of the Christian faith that all are in need of healing, all are disciples or 'learners', and that charity is not to be confused with 'fixing' things, but rather with *com*passion, literally suffering with, those who, *like us*, are in need. By this reckoning, theologically-informed 'social liturgy' becomes much more about the church's ability to welcome people into transformative relationships than simply addressing their needs or performing acts of charitable service.[27]

The way in which such social liturgy is incarnated will differ from one activity and one situation to another, but in order to avoid slipping into 'mere' social action, it will need to think carefully about how it is different. A few criteria for this 'framing' are discussed in the next section.

# framing social liturgy

## the authenticity of social liturgy

Christians do not have the monopoly on social action, as they themselves are usually the first to admit. Innumerable other groups within contemporary society are engaged in healing and helping, advising and instructing.

*All social action should ideally be authentic, true to its own motivations, and that is no less the case for social liturgy.*

The reasons for such action are complex and various. Some people get engaged through a sense of duty, some through an experience of loss, some through a stake in the local community, some through a surfeit of spare time, some for more explicitly religious reasons. Recognising the legitimacy of such a wide range of motivations is essential as it helps guard against the deadening idea that all social action is, or at least should be, inspired by depersonalised and disinterested motivations, and which sees a 'hidden agenda' in anything that appears to deviate from this supposed norm.

Such an understanding is perilous. It would be crass to accuse the mother who was involved in local community action of really doing so because she wanted to make life in their neighbourhood better for her children. It would be worse to accuse the father who lost a child to mental illness of setting up a mental health charity only to enable him to cope with the grief. People engage in social action for any number, or combination, of reasons: duty, enlightened self-interest, personal need, undiluted selflessness, and religious conviction. So it is that we should hope and expect Christians to get engaged simply because they are Christians. All social action should ideally be authentic, true to its own motivations, and that is no less the case for social liturgy.

The reason this matters is well articulated in Catholic Social Thought. In his 1967 encyclical *Populorum progressio* ('The Development of Peoples'), Pope Paul VI observed that "every form of social action involves some doctrine."[28] In other words, what organisations do and how they do it almost invariably embodies some imprint of *why* they are acting. The authenticity of social action is important not simply because it offers the respect due to those engaged in such action, but because it enables a rich variety of different approaches to different social needs, recognising that just as one size needn't fit all, nor does one motivation.

> What organisations do and how they do it almost invariably embodies some imprint of why they are acting.

Paul VI went on to explain that "the Christian rejects that which is based on a materialistic and atheistic philosophy, namely one which shows no respect for a religious outlook on life, for freedom or human dignity",[29] the implication being that a purely materialistic conception of the human good is in danger of ignoring less tangible goods (e.g. spiritual, relational or emotional ones) and constricting intellectual and religious freedom (in much the same way as an unduly 'spiritual' one could downplay material goods). Social liturgy should be *Christian* because that element brings with it particular ideas, commitments and nuances that will contribute to the good they are seeking to achieve.[30]

Paul VI's statement on social action and doctrine was picked up by Benedict XVI, who quoted it in his 2009 encyclical *Caritas in Veritate* ('Charity in Truth'), which revisited Paul VI's earlier work. In the same vein, Benedict also wrote, in his earlier encyclical *Deus caritas est* ('God is love'), that "it is very important that the Church's charitable activity maintains all of its splendour and does not become just another form of social assistance".[31]

This encyclical proceeded to outline the "distinctiveness" of the church's charitable activity, remarking that those who work in such activity "must be distinguished by the fact that they do not merely meet the needs of the moment, but they dedicate themselves to others with heartfelt concern, enabling them to experience the richness of their humanity." Social liturgy should, in other words, bear the visible mark of love of the gospel:

> In addition to their necessary professional training, these charity workers need a "formation of the heart": they need to be led to that encounter with God in Christ which awakens their love and opens their spirits to others. As a result, love

of neighbour will no longer be for them a commandment imposed, so to speak, from without, but a consequence deriving from their faith, a faith which becomes active through love (cf. Gal 5:6).[32]

Social liturgy should be *authentically* Christian, marked, among other things, by commitment, love and recognition of the personal nature of all social encounters.

*Social liturgy should bear the visible mark of love of the gospel.*

Is it? In one respect this question is unanswerable. Motivations are not always obvious and hardly ever single or exclusive. That said, we have already cited a few examples of Christian organisations that seem to illustrate this kind of "liturgical" authenticity. The work of Christians Against Poverty is profoundly pastoral as well as being practical and professional. The remarkable story of the L'Arche community embodies a view of the world marked by dignity and mutuality. Each person is understood as a unrepeatable gift[33] and this involves not only the idea that people are a gift from God and that their dignity should be recognised and affirmed irrespective of their cognitive capacity, but also that people with diminished cognitive capacity have themselves something to give to others; hence the principle of those with profoundly different levels of cognitive ability *living together.*[34]

The Street Pastors/City Angels initiatives deal with people in very different states of need and are noteworthy in many ways, such as their practical responses[35] and their evangelistic sensitivity.[36] However, perhaps most remarkable is the manner in which some very unlikely people find themselves in situations of menace and even potential violence in the nightlife of many cities, their presence diffusing tension and aggression in a way that the police find very difficult to do. In effect, this is an example of 'peacemaking' in a creative if unfamiliar way.

Other examples multiply. The Archbishop of Canterbury's own initiative, the Community of St Anselm, based in Lambeth, is a classic example of social liturgy, "follow[ing] the Franciscan insight that becoming more like Jesus is inseparable from serving others."[37] A number of the organisations studied in the Plater Trust/Theos report on Catholic charities in the UK today, such as the Saint Vincent de Paul Society or Father Hudson's Care, the social care agency for the Archdiocese of Birmingham, embodied key principles from Catholic Social Teaching, like 'the option for the poor', 'solidarity', and 'personalism' in their activities, in the process transforming social action into social liturgy. The parish churches studied as part of the Theos research for the Church Urban Fund were marked by an emphasis on relationality (people could not thrive outside of caring and secure relationships), hospitality (constantly emphasising the welcome of the other in community buildings, in church services or relationships), hopefulness and incarnation (offering an ongoing presence in communities spanning generations, even when circumstances were not auspicious). The work of Sanctus St Mark's in Stoke on Trent is another example, in the way it supports asylum seekers and refugees as "a reflection of the self giving love of Jesus Christ [with a welcome which] aims to be open, non-judgemental and generous, treating all people with equality and dignity, regardless of their economic or social circumstances."[38] All of these in their own way reflect and embody deep theological commitments and values in their activities, demonstrating authentically Christian ways of "Doing Good".

It is through examples such as these, and many others, that the Christian response to the social challenges articulated in chapter two is to be found; not in the finger-pointing, Bible-bashing, puritanical (and often hypocritical) moralizing of the popular imagination but through authentic Christian social liturgy. A significant range of such activities are already operated by, through and in churches, often focussing on the key relational building blocks of people's lives through, for example, marriage preparation and "enrichment" courses, 'New Beginnings' courses (helping people recover and move on from divorce and separation), bereavement counselling, and family, children and youth services. These are long-standing church interests. More recently, more churches and Christian charities are getting engaged in issues of happiness,[39] anxiety and depression,[40] mental health,[41] disabilities,[42] alcohol and drug addiction,[43] and many of the other problems briefly outlined in chapter two.

We should not exaggerate how 'recent' this activity is. *Mutatis mutandis*, as already pointed out earlier in this essay, churches and Christian charities were doing precisely this work, to a herculean extent, in the Victorian period; and indeed organisations like the Salvation Army never stopped. Nor should we imagine that authentic Christian social liturgy will always look, sound or feel the same. The Theos report *The Problem of Proselytism* pointed out that faith-based agencies could and did adopt different 'levels' of faith-identity.[44]

Rather, the point is that figures appear to show a growing engagement in precisely the social and relational issues that vex contemporary Britain, which is motivated and informed by open and authentic Christian commitments.

## the practice of social liturgy

Pope Paul VI's statement, quoted above, that "every form of social action involves some doctrine" gestures towards a second, linked consideration. Just as it is important to think through the *why* of social liturgy, it is essential to think through the *how*.

The case study research we conducted for the Church Urban Fund showed that it wasn't simply how many people the churches came into contact with that was noteworthy, or even the range of 'services' provided, but the *persistent*, *relational* and *localised* way such contact was pursued.

Churches and key staff were commonly trusted by local elected representatives, by community partners, and by those who worked with them – but they were trusted because the institution was there for the long haul. One interviewee, for example, recalled the lukewarm response her Community Project first received from local people, not because they didn't want or even appreciate the services offered, but because they said they had seen similar projects (though not, in those instances, church projects) come and go with depressing regularity. Funding cycles were short, grants were not renewed, projects ended abruptly, and community workers left the area. This time, they felt, would be no different. Twenty-years later, this particular interviewee, who still led the community project (despite, as it happens, now suffering from terminal cancer) could testify to the difference such persistence had made. Persistence of this kind spoke not simply of a well-meaning professional delivering goods to those in need, but of fellow humans living, working and forming deep personal relationships with other people. Trust, often spoken about but less often embodied, was no easy sentiment, but a virtue born of hard persistence, and social liturgy has to establish legitimacy to speak of it, by remaining with the people they serve, rather than being vulnerable to the vicissitudes of short-term funding cycles.

Second, this persistence was a persistence of relationships. Churches promoted and embodied 'neighbourliness', the physical edifice of the church and the regular worshipping community that met in it enabling those in the wider community to build relationships of mutual support that helped people, families and communities develop resilience in the face of social and economic challenges. Interviewees in the Catholic Charities project spoke of "do[ing] compassion, as in the real meaning of the word compassion – suffering with". "It's not enough to give money," another interviewee, from the Saint Vincent de Paul Society (SVP), explained. "Real charity is befriending and getting alongside people." This, however, could be costly. "It hurts more," a third interviewee claimed. "That's the truth. When someone dies or goes off the rails it hurts that much more because you actually knew them."[45] Relationality, like trust, was hard won, but a key characteristic of Christian social activity.

Third was the local knowledge. Churches ran a range of community projects, many of which were developed and adapted as a bespoke response to a particular local need, such as a children's clothing exchange, English language courses, debt counselling and access to credit unions, or lunch clubs for older people. Catholic charities frequently interacted with parish structures to draw on local volunteers and expertise as a means of accessing and responding to the community's needs, and although 'subsidiarity' was not well understood as a term, there was a strong theme of the importance of finding local solutions to local problems.

Such 'localism' didn't mean that projects would necessarily be different. In the words of one interviewee, "many of the local problems are the same and the solutions are often obvious – food, clothing, shelter and friendship. Not every project has to be incredibly exciting to be what's needed." Nonetheless, the localised and embodied nature of the social action often meant that nuances and particularities of a context could be grasped and engaged if needed.

Persistence, relationality and localised engagement: these were just three ways in which the authentically Christian nature of these forms of social engagement could (not, of course, always did) manifest itself. Others – such as an emphasis on hospitality, or hopefulness, or unconditional acceptance – might also apply.

This is not a template for social liturgy.[46] Indeed, there is no possible template for it: different incarnations of this kind of social action will differ in various ways. The point being made here is that just as those Christians and churches motivated to serve their communities will do so for authentic theological motivations, they will also do so in ways that embody – that really live out – those motivations.

## the account of social liturgy

Knowing the logic the underpins social liturgy and enabling that to inform what and how it is done, leads us to a third, key consideration: honesty. The questions 'why are you doing this?' and 'why are you doing this in this way?' merit answers, and they are ones that are easier to get wrong than to get right. Two pitfalls stand out.

The first is denial. For fear of provoking secular wrath, or for reasons of old-fashioned British embarrassment and reticence when it comes to talking about religion, or simply because one doesn't have a well-thought through explanation, the temptation is to deny there are any particular motivations to be explained or to mumble something noncommittal, vague and studiously inoffensive. While there is nothing culpable in doing this, it remains an inadequate and ultimately dishonest response. If Christians are doing this because of their Christian faith, they owe it others to say so.

That, however, can easily send them across the spectrum into the other pitfall which is seeing the curious question as an invitation to deliver a sermon or apologetic lecture. Just because someone is interested to find out more, that doesn't necessarily mean that they are *that* interested, and the ham-fisted answer is undoubtedly worse than the vague and noncommittal one.

Ultimately, it is incumbent upon those engaged in social liturgy always to be prepared to give an answer to everyone who asks for the reason for the hope they are trying to bring to a person's, family's or community's life. The echo of 1 Peter 3:15 is obvious here, and intentional, as the idea of living in such a way as would provoke curiosity among others runs straight back into the New Testament.[47] If the reason and practice of social liturgy is authentically Christian it should provoke questions.

> It is precisely being able to locate and articulate the theological heartbeat of such social activity – of keeping it tethered to the good news of the kingdom of God – that will prevent it from going the same way as the old Social Gospel.

This is not the place to outline the answer to be given, except to say that there will be no such thing as *the* answer: different activities by different people with different people in different places will have different 'theological' explanations. That recognised, the very idea of Christian social liturgy (as opposed to the Social Gospel) is that any account offered will sidestep the fault line that there has sometimes been between the 'Social' (feeding, clothing, helping, visiting, etc.) and 'Gospel' (praying, singing, hoping for heaven, etc.). Christian social liturgy is love of God in love of neighbour, worship as service. Indeed, it is not too much of an exaggeration to say that it is precisely being able to locate and articulate the theological heartbeat of such social activity – of keeping it tethered to the good news of the kingdom of God – that will prevent it from going the same way as the old Social Gospel.

So it is that an account of social liturgy may dwell on the Sermon on the Mount, or the parables, or the self-giving of the crucifixion, or the hope of the resurrection, or the moral exhortation of the apostles, or the communal life of a worshipping community, or a sense of obedience and duty to God, or a response to the love experienced from God, or some combination of these, or something else altogether. But whatever it is, it must recognise a vision of the human good in which material and spiritual are thoroughly intertwined.

## answering concerns

If there is real potential in the idea of social liturgy, there are also problems – or at least potential problems. As religious groups have come to play an ever greater role in the provision of 'services' which, in the recent past (though not, of course, in the longer view) have been deemed the provenance of the (supposedly neutral, 'secular') state, a number voices have raised concerns. These come in a variety of ways (and in a variety of tones, from the acute and considered to the ignorant and hysterical). In the remainder of this chapter, I will look at four common ones – concerning the problems of proselytism, pluralism, public legitimacy and public reasoning – and explore how the idea of social liturgy speaks to each of them.

## the problem of proselytism

The very idea that social liturgy is central to the future of Christianity in the UK will raise the eyebrows, or indeed the hackles, of some secularists. Is this not a plain admission, the cry comes back, that so-called social liturgy is not an end in itself but merely a means of growing the church, a Trojan Horse wheeled into unsuspecting communities out of which creep dozens of heavily-armed evangelists at nightfall? Isn't social liturgy merely proselytism by another name?

This accusation may be compounded by the (little) research done in this area which suggests that churches do in fact grow as a consequence of social action. Analysis of the 2012 and 2014 National Church and Social Action Surveys, undertaken by Jubilee+, suggests that "church-based social action initiatives are perceived to have a positive impact on church growth, in terms of people being added to local congregations, as well as being a social good."[48] The extent of that impact is far from uniform and varies "according to factors such as the type and duration of social action and church size and location." However, this does not change the basic conclusion and effectively intensifies the problem, for if there is one thing worse than proselytism that is dressed up as social liturgy, it is successful proselytism that is dressed up as social liturgy.[49]

The first thing to say about this concern is that it is not illegitimate. The idea of social action as an exchange for or, worse, disguised compulsion to, piety is not simply the creation of the secularist's over-fertile imagination. That acknowledged, there are two oft-cited and substantial responses to this accusation that bear careful repeating. The first is that such an approach is explicitly and repeatedly censured in Christian teaching. In the Sermon on the Mount, Christ is about as clear on the dynamics of gift and service as it is possible to be. Those who claim to follow him should not give with strings attached. Generosity should be generosity, not a covert exchange, whether for favours, social approval or converts. Those who give to the needy should not even let their left hand know what their right hand is doing (Matt 6:1-4). "Freely you have received; freely give," he tells them later.[50] The New Testament epistles strike a similar note. Giving, even giving generously, is not enough if not marked by love, Paul tells the church in Corinth (1 Cor. 13:3). "Each of you should use whatever gift you have received to serve others," Peter writes in 1 Peter 4:10.

Such instructions are made still more explicit in contemporary church teaching. In a similar vein, but more closely focused on contemporary concerns, Benedict XVI was quite explicit that charity work cannot be used for "what is nowadays called proselytism".[51] "Love is free; it is not practised as a way of achieving other ends."[52] There may well be Christians who engage in social action for the sake of bums on seats, but in doing so they are directly contravening church teaching.

The fact is, however, that there don't appear to be many such Christians. This leads us to our second response. What empirical evidence there is suggests that these principles are largely obeyed in practice. A detailed study into 'The difference that "faith" makes: faith-based organisations and the provision of services for homeless people', part of AHRC/ ESRC's Religion and Society programme found that, in contradiction to presumptions that Faith Based Organisations "try to convert service users or make moralistic demands of them", "FBOs did not 'force' religion onto homeless people, and very rarely demanded particular behavioural changes." The study concluded that:

> the common distrust of FBOs which endures in the sector is misplaced and founded on outdated views of faith-based provision[;] there was no evidence that FBOs used such funds to propagate religion, or excluded potential users on grounds such as religious belief or sexual orientation [and that] these findings should allay concerns about the propriety of using public funds to support faith-based services.[53]

Similar findings were confirmed by the Theos research project *The Problem of Proselytism*.[54]

Neither of these arguments, of course, indicates that there *could* never be a problem with proselytism but they strongly suggest that it is far less of a problem than some imagine. If anything, as *The Problem of Proselytism* argues, social liturgy groups tend more to "experience pressures which can *prevent* them from maintaining a strong religious ethos and offering services which give due regard to spiritual care."[55] As we shall note below, such a suppression of religious identity would be not only problematic itself, but ultimately counter-productive.

Should those engaged in social liturgy seek, then, to make 'disciples'? The answer to this is less fraught than is sometimes assumed. It is that such action should aim to do what it is there to do – help, heal, counsel, feed, clothe, etc. – and to be open about the theological reason behind it. If that intrigues and engages people who then proceed to ask questions and enquire about Christianity – good: that is the right moment to respond intelligently and sensitively to any questions asked. If, conversely, it does not intrigue and engage people, who move on without ever wondering about Christianity – good: a genuine human need has still been served and a public good achieved. Social liturgy should not be shy of conversations about Christianity, which often plant seeds that may grow disciples and congregations – but it should remember that in the context of their action these are 'supplementary' goods, commendable results but never the *objective* of such action.[56]

## the problem of pluralism

This leads to a second concern often voiced about social liturgy. The UK is now a more plural nation than it was a generation or two ago, not least religiously plural. Does not having specifically religiously-inspired projects, so the rhetorical question goes, risk destabilising that pluralism and fracturing the (fragile?) concord that underpins any society that is criss-crossed by substantive differences?

The original *"Doing God"* report highlighted this concern, in a subsection on the potential 'sectarianism' of public religiosity, and cited theoretical and practical examples of how this fear was either exaggerated or, if not exaggerated, could be circumvented. As an example, it quoted a 2006 House of Lords debate on the role of the churches in the civic life of towns and cities, in which the Muslim peer Lord Ahmed said of his experience working with the church when he was a councillor in Rotherham, that it was

> one of the most wonderful experiences, for a Church leader, a local councillor and the local mayor all to be seen going together when there was tension to visit communities where we were able to give the impression that we can all work together to bring harmony and equality for our communities.[57]

In this instance, the particular religious affiliations involved in the social action were not threats to the cultural pluralism of Rotherham, but reflections of it, and recognising them "helped to empower the local community and to deal with deprivation."[58]

Since then there have been many examples of how Christian public action has worked to calm, rather than provoke, community tensions, with the 2013 Theos report, *Making Multiculturalism Work* putting further empirical evidence on the theoretical bones. This study examined two live initiatives – community organising and Near Neighbours – as examples of how 'political friendships' are formed and sustained within communities that are marked by 'deep diversity'. Rather than relying on complex theories of multi- or inter-culturalism, the report argued that it was "ordinary relationships" forged by people who were on different sides of various religious and cultural divides, but who worked together for local common goods that best built secure community cohesion. 'Side-by-side' activity was often more productive than 'face-to-face' discussion.

Crucially, this was not 'side-by-side' activity that had first been shorn of its religious or cultural particularities and compelled to satisfy some 'progressive test', whereby groups were required to show that they are sufficiently politically progressive in order to merit a 'place at the table'. Such an approach was found to be not only illiberal but also counter-productive, killing off the potential for friendship across difference and encouraging retrenchment rather than transformation. Rather, the study commended a 'relational test', whereby "the central criterion for participation is that an organisation must show that it is willing and able to work with people from different backgrounds and perspectives".

*Making Multiculturalism Work* argued that what it termed 'political friendships' – relationships of genuine trust and mutuality forged in a plural public square – not only could be but needed to be open and honest about people's motivations and objectives. Friendships that were deaf to people's core identity, values and motivations were destined to be superficial or insincere.

This would not necessarily be easy. Indeed, on the contrary, it is arguably easier to circumvent or bury difference at the outset, so as to avoid awkward or problematic differences from intruding into common tasks. Such is the logic of secularism, at least in its more palatable forms.[59] However, just as many theorists have come to the conclusion that, in Richard Rorty's words, "attempts to find rules that are neutral between the two sides [religious and secular] are pretty hopeless [as is] the attempt to say that one or another contribution to political discourse is illegitimate,"[60] so our research suggests it is potentially counterproductive.

> The answer is not secularism, which falls short on so many levels, but appropriately watchful and cautious honesty and authenticity.

The implication of this for social liturgy, any ideologically-motivated social action, is significant, and in line with that outlined in the previous section on proselytism. Just because social liturgy should be able to be secure in its identity, without fear of secular accusations of divisiveness or sectarianism, it doesn't mean that it has to wear its heart on its sleeve. The Theos report on proselytism offered a typology of faith-based organisations (full-, half-, and low-fat) to clarify their different 'levels' or intensities of religious ethos. The typology applies just as well here, as some forms of social liturgy will, for whatever reason, wish to sit very loosely to their Christian identity, whereas others will want it to be deep and pervasive. The point here is not to adjudicate between different types of action and decide which is more authentic and which less. Rather it is to answer the basic concern pertaining to religiously-inspired social action in a plural society and suggest that the answer is not secularism, which falls short on so many levels, but appropriately watchful and cautious honesty and authenticity.

The Brexit referendum and result exposed some deep and alarming tensions and antagonisms within British society (most of which, it might be noted as an aside, have little to do with 'religion'). We dismiss worries about the fragility of a plural society at some risk. Yet the proper response to this is not to bury difference, or to force it onto some secular Procrustean bed, or to deny it entry into public life altogether, but to acknowledge, admit and avail ourselves of it, all the time attending to the challenges that come with it.

# the problem of public legitimacy

Advocating social liturgy as central to the future of Christianity in Britain has the advantage of speaking into a third vexed debate around the role of 'religion' in public life. If 'proselytism' deals with concerns over illegitimate social action, and 'pluralism' with concerns of the potentially harmful side-effects of such action, the problem of public legitimacy deals with the wider concern over who has a 'right' to speak into public debate at all.

On the theoretical surface, this is not a concern at all. Indeed, it is precisely one of the key characteristics of a liberal society that everyone has a right to speak up and put forth their point of view. In reality, however, the question of who has the right to be *heard*, the right actually to inform and shape our common life, is a genuine, live and rather more vexed one.

This is a particular issue for the church or, more precisely, the established church, simply by dint of its establishment. Although possibly not quite the unadulterated privilege that its critics think it is, the very fact that the establishment of a church that attracts around two per cent of the population each Sunday attracts so much criticism is testimony to the fact that there is an issue here.

The error of this debate, however, is that it too readily gravitates to the other pole which says that because the established church, or Christians in general, only comprise a minority of the population now, they have obviously forfeited their right to seriously shape our common life, which should properly be the right of the other 90%.

The problem with this argument is that there is no "other 90%". For one thing, one cannot discard Christian nominalism quite as readily as that. The fact that somewhere around 15 million adults call themselves Christians even if many rarely darken the door of a church is not immaterial and if it denotes anything it is surely that they have some kind of loose sympathy with the Christian worldview.

More importantly, however, the other 90%, or the other 60%, does not comprise a homogenous whole, whose view is coherent and consistent. This is not simply a question of the many millions of religious minorities living in Britain (who, in any case, don't necessarily agree with one another), but the obvious (but all-too-often ignored) point that the non-religious group is not homogenous. Given that the membership levels of the various anti-religious societies in the UK – secularist, humanist, atheist – number in their thousands, it would be brave to claim that they spoke for the 25 million people who don't call themselves religious.

The 2014 Theos report *Voting and Values* illustrated how complex and diverse is not only British public opinion and values, on so many issues, but also how complexly that mapped out onto concepts of religiosity.[61] It showed that Christians, people of other faiths, and the non-religious could be found clustered in different ways on the various different axes – left-right, libertarian-authoritarian, welfarist-individualist – that describe contemporary public opinion. There was little sense that Christian public opinion was somehow out-of-step with that of the rest of public opinion: there was no such thing as 'Christian public opinion' and certainly no such thing as non-Christian or non-religious public opinion.

The result of all this is a degree of confusion about which we instinctively feel uncomfortable. If we shouldn't particularly 'listen' to Christian (or religious) views because they are a minority (and hardly a unanimous one at that), nor should we 'listen' to 'the rest of public opinion' because that simply invites the question: which part of 'the rest of public opinion' should we attend to? Is the only fair option a straightforward aggregation of individual opinions, a kind of democratic populism, government by referendum? Is there any public legitimacy beyond having more people who have voted for you than for others?

*It is those who are doing good – irrespective of whether they are also doing God – who merit most attention in a plural public square such as ours.*

The answer proposed by this essay is yes, and that such public legitimacy is grounded in active, tangible and (ideally) measurable contribution to the wider public good. For all that people formed by different cultural and ideological commitments will disagree about the nature (and even the existence) of a common good, the practical reality tends to be different. Few people actively think that it is wrong to visit the lonely, look after children, provide lunch clubs for the elderly, offer support to the bereaved, provide rehabilitation for addicts, steer drunks from the gutter, give up space for community ventures, support asylum seekers, and host foodbanks, jobs clubs, and debt advice centres. Such activities show a concrete commitment to the public good that you have to try very hard to deny.

On this logic, public legitimacy is, if not formally predicated on, at least informed by concrete commitment to a palpable public good. The answer to the question 'why should we pay any (special) attention to what you say?' lies not in the fact of establishment *per se*, nor in the fiction that the non-religious view is homogenous and represented by vocal secular groups, but rather in the demonstrable fact of contributing to the public good. It is those who are doing good – irrespective of whether they are also doing God – who merit most attention in a plural public square such as ours.

# the problem of public reasoning

The problem of public reasoning is naturally closely linked to that of public legitimacy; indeed, in one sense it is a subset of it. However, it is different enough to merit a separate point, not least seeing as the question of 'inaccessibility' was raised in the original *"Doing God"* essay, as one of the more coherent reasons against the presence of religion in public life.

This pointed out that there was a legitimate concern about the kind of religious reasoning in public life that draws explicitly on authorities – textual (e.g. the Bible) or institutional (e.g. papal) – that are not shared by other people. However, it also pointed out that such reasoning tends to be unsupported by the evidence. As the Theos report *Coming off the Bench*[62] showed, bishops in the Lords may have been more active in the Blair years than in the Thatcher ones, but only rarely drew on the Bible or explicit (and allegedly alienating) theological reasoning when doing so. The 'because the Bible/the Pope/the Holy Spirit says so' argument is something of a straw man.

More importantly, however, the idea that there is some neutral and universally acceptable reasoning – Rawls' "proper political reasons" to be deployed instead of or alongside the unacceptable "comprehensive doctrines" – is a myth. *"Doing God"* quoted Julian Baggini, one of the acutest and most generous atheist critics writing in Britain today, making the Rawlsian point that for all that a devout Catholic will be strongly influenced by her religious beliefs on a subject like abortion, and for all that such belief will naturally and legitimately come through when speaking in a civic forum such as Parliament, "vitally, she must find some way of expressing them in terms that everyone can understand and appreciate." The problem with this position, reasonable as it sounds, however, is what makes us think that there will be significant agreement between different parties on major political or moral issues, let alone contentious ones like abortion? The fear that has sometimes been voiced about this is that the idea that X must express herself in terms that 'everyone' can understand and appreciate, actually means X must express herself in terms that secular liberals can understand. And that is to try and win the argument without actually arguing it.

Building on these ideas, Jonathan Chaplin's carefully-argued report, *Talking God: The legitimacy of religious public reasoning*,[63] rightly recognised that we should expect *dissensus* rather than *consensus*, not least about debateable issues (the clue is in the name) in the public square. There is no 'everyone' from whom we should expect principled agreement concerning the foundations, logic and language of our argument. In this way, liberal secularism, while priding itself on making space for pluralism, in fact "contains unacknowledged exclusivist tendencies that work to close down legitimate diversity."[64] Moreover, there are good reasons to believe that it is perfectly legitimate to offer explicitly *religious* reasons in presenting public justifications for laws or public policies (although legitimate does not necessarily mean sensible or advisable). Chaplin outlines the circumstances in which such reasoning might be more or less acceptable, but the overall thrust is that public reasoning must pay due attention to the genuinely plural conceptual nature of the public square.

There is a danger here, which some critics raise, that this threatens to dissolve public debate into mutually-incomprehensible silos, 'public discourses of the deaf' as it were. While this may be something of a counsel of despair, it is nonetheless true that not only should we not expect agreement on key issues (start and end of life being the most obvious today), but nor should we expect agreement on how to talk about them. Our differences go all the way down.

That duly noted, an important but largely overlooked element in the discussion of public reasoning is how such discussions are embedded in actual practices and modes of life. Put another way, while it is inevitable that people will argue for and against different positions on these contentious issues, if all they are doing is *arguing* about them, they risk missing the reality of the lives and situations involved. Arguments need to be grounded in practices.

One way of looking at this is to say it is one thing to be pro-life and quite another to be pro-life and simultaneously to provide counselling, parenting, and if necessary adoption services. It is one thing to make principled arguments against assisted dying, and other to make the same arguments in the context of extensive end-of-life care and the Hospice Movement. It is one thing to make arguments about policing and urban security, another to make the same arguments in the context of the Street Pastor movement; one thing to make arguments about cuts and taxation, another to do so in the context of debt advice and foodbanks.

> In a public discourse in which different people with different ideologies will often be talking past one another, concrete social action is the closest thing we may have to a lingua franca.

To be clear: just because an institution (and in his instance it doesn't matter whether that institution is Christian, Muslim, or secular) is delivering a palpable good through society, that doesn't mean that its theoretical arguments on that particular topic should win through. 'Doing Good' is no substitute for serious arguments and clashing of ideas in the public square. Rather, it is to emphasise that arguments are not just arguments but are about people and problems, and that those arguments that are clearly built on concrete responses to genuine needs should have a particular legitimacy in public debate. Ultimately, in a public discourse in which different people with different ideologies will often be talking past one another, concrete social action is the closest thing we may have to a *lingua franca*.

## conclusion: doing God by doing good

This essay has argued that, for all the challenges facing Christianity in contemporary Britain, there are reasons to be encouraged. The powerful growth of Christian social liturgy over recent years, in response to the real, deep, sometimes widespread and seemingly growing social problems explored in chapter two, is not only encouraging in itself, but a healthy redirection from understanding Christianity as simply a system of belief or narrowly-conceived worship to understanding it as a full enactment of the Kingdom of God that Jesus came announcing.

The potential is enormous, but so are the challenges.

Work is needed to encourage churches and Christian groups to see social liturgy as central to their common life and worship, to understand how the church community might live and work alongside those with particular needs and concerns that may not be visible on a Sunday morning. Research is needed to help them identify and understand the dynamics of their areas, and to enable them to develop and sustain viable models of social action; ideally every church should be known by those in their community as the place where their true humanity is recognised and affirmed. Work is also needed to encourage people to tithe their time and talents as well as (or perhaps instead of) their money to such activities, which are as much in need of IT, legal, and administrative support as they are of more obviously pastoral roles – ideally every believer, no matter how 'irrelevant' they judge their personal and professional talents, should have a role in their church's social liturgy.

> ideally every believer, no matter how 'irrelevant' they judge their personal and professional talents, should have a role in their church's social liturgy.

Beyond these practical considerations, work is needed to theoretically – or theologically – ground them. We need to think carefully about how to help ensure that social liturgy does not slide into becoming social action; to help churches root their activities in their faith, to shape it accordingly, to equip them to explain what they are doing, and to prevent them from diluting or ignoring that basic theological DNA if they meet with incomprehension or hostility. Ideally every church should be conscious of how their social liturgy is an intentional and careful worship of God.

What this looks like in practice is hard to say and hard to generalise about, though the William Temple Foundation has fruitfully explored what that which it calls 'social capital' might look like in reality. Their list includes wanting to transform people personally and spiritually, as well as materially or physically; consciously accepting people who have been rejected elsewhere; valuing personal stories about how personal and corporate regeneration occurs; introducing values of self-emptying, forgiveness, transformation, and openness to learning into the experience; acknowledging and respecting the fact that strong and negative personal emotions are part of the experience of transformation; valuing (indeed expecting) people's own inner resources and their capacity to create their own solutions to problems; and believing, implicitly or explicitly, that God is already at work within these examples of regeneration and transformation.

Finally, work is needed to make political and public space for such social liturgy. Better religious literacy is needed to calm secular nerves and to show the genuine public good that is served by such social liturgy. Careful legal and jurisprudential work is needed to ensure that the deadening hand of (the more muscular kinds of) secularism doesn't squeeze the authentic Christian motivations out of such action. We need to dismantle fears around bogey words like proselytism and show how, in reality, social liturgy as discussed in this essay is not a threat to a liberal order, but a reflection of it, and one that helps us navigate such vexed issues as public legitimacy and public reasoning.

It is, in short, a big ask. But to do it would not only help change the script about Christianity in contemporary Britain but also, perhaps, bring the life of churches close to that of the earliest church – operating in a plural, often incomprehending, and sometimes hostile environment, which it managed, ultimately, to tame and change through its determination to believe in and live out a story of forgiveness, generosity and love.

# chapter 3 – references

1    The data here tend to be less robust than those for other areas.

2    David Bull, Lucy de Las Casas and Rachel Wharton, *Faith Matters: Understanding the size, income and focus of faith-based charities* (NPC, June 2016).

3    Bull et al, *Faith Matters*, Table 9.

4    Paul Bickley, *Good Neighbours: How Churches Help Communities Flourish* (Theos, 2014); http://www.theosthinktank.co.uk/publications/2014/07/10/good-neighbours-how-churches-help-communities-flourish

5    Note: this is the church in England not solely the Church of England.

6    http://www.cinnamonnetwork.co.uk/wp-content/uploads/2015/05/Final-National-Report.pdf

7    As the British Religion in Numbers coverage of this research did point out, however, this sample was recruited through the invitation of local champions and may not be statistically representative. Figures at this level should always be treated with caution but with that duly noted, there is no doubting the sheer volume of social activity detected by the survey.

8    http://www.jubilee-plus.org/Articles/431253/Jubilee_Plus/Research/RESULTS_OF_THE.aspx

9    Up to age 11, excluding church's own children's ministry.

10   Again, apart from the church's own members.

11   Aged 12-18, again excluding the churches' own youth ministry.

12   Other services included initiatives distributing clothes, helping with fitness, helping adults with special needs, giving mental health/stress counselling, delivering English as a second language courses, running social enterprises, helping with adoption, and helping sex workers/trafficking.

13   And increased it by the improbably high 59.4% compared with four years ago.

14   And by 36.5% in four years.

15   The study calculated that this would amount to £2.4 billion p/a, which increased to £3.5 billion, "if we then include the use of facilities and direct financial contributions". It also noted that "*the figures only cover Church social action initiatives, and did not include voluntary work by Christians in the community that is not initiated by a church (e.g. work by local charities)*".

16   Piketty, *Capital*, p. 481.

17   Frank Prochaska, *Schools of Citizenship: Charity and Civic Value* (London: Civitas, 2002), pp. 41-48.

18   Piketty, *Capital*, p. 173.

19   Piketty, *Capital*, p. 93.

20   It is a curious fact, and one certainly worth noting as an aside, that the institutional churches in Britain have been at the forefront of criticisms against governments that have purposed to rein in state spending, from the much-vaunted *Faith in the City* report of 1985 to episcopal condemnations of austerity thirty years later. See, for example, Jason Beattie, '27 bishops

slam David Cameron's welfare reforms as creating a national crisis in unprecedented attack', *Daily Mirror*, 19 February 2014, http://www.mirror.co.uk/news/uk-news/27-bishops-slam-david-camerons-3164033#ixzz3FRc0At3V; End Hunger Fast Press Release, 'Church leaders call national fast for UK's hungry as "End Hunger Fast" campaign planned for Lent', 19 February 2014, http://endhungerfast.co.uk/campaign-press-release-church-leaders-call-national-fast-uks-hungry-end-hunger-fast-campaign-planned-lent/ ; John Bingham, 'New Cardinal Vincent Nichols: welfare cuts 'frankly a disgrace'', *Daily Telegraph*, 14 February 2014, http://www.telegraph.co.uk/news/religion/10639015/New-Cardinal-Vincent-Nichols-welfare-cuts-frankly-a-disgrace.html No one could accuse the institutional churches of agitating for a smaller state so that they might have a bigger role. Not without irony could Peter Kellner argue in *Prospect* magazine that the "the Church of England should abandon religion and become a political party." https://yougov.co.uk/news/2013/12/20/christmas-thought-church-england/

21   http://www.bbc.co.uk/news/world-europe-21793224

22   Luke 1:23

23   Hebrews 8:6

24   2 Corinthians 9:12. I am grateful to Jon Riding for helping me understand the meaning of this complex word in greater detail, and also alerting me to nuances that I have not gone into here.

25   Philippians 2:30

26   Philippians 2:17

27   I am grateful to Bethany Eckley for helping me think through these issues.

28   *Populorum Progressio*, #39.

29   *Populorum Progressio*, #39.

30   Particular, it is important to note here, does not mean unique. There is nothing in Christian social action that says such an approach is unachievable for non-Christians, just as the same applies vice versa. No doubt there will be times when such action is distinctive and different, but that is to be celebrated rather than safeguarded. The call, however, is for authentic rather than distinctive social action, activity that honours the ideas and commitments that drive it and in so doing brings something particular to enrich our common life.

31   *Caritas in Veritate*, #31.

32   *Caritas in Veritate*, #31a.

33   cf. Pope Benedict's words in *Caritas in Veritate* (#34) that "the human being is made for gift".

34   For more details see http://www.larche.org.uk/

35   E.g. carrying flip-flops for those who might otherwise turn an ankle in the stagger home.

36   E.g. Never initiating a faith conversation but always responding to one.

37   http://stanselm.org.uk/

38   http://www.sanctusstmarks.co.uk/

39  The Christian charity Livability runs a specific "Happiness Course": http://www.livability.org. uk/blog-and-resources/training-and-events/the-happiness-course/

40  For an example of one such course see http://www.saintpauls.co.uk/Groups/245354/ Exploring_Anxiety_and.aspx

41  For example, http://www.crosswayscommunity.co.uk/

42  For example, http://www.throughtheroof.org/ and (again) http://www.livability.org.uk/

43  For example, http://www.betel.uk/ and http://www.remar.uk.com/

44  The report suggests three categories: (1) *Full fat*, where "it's not possible to abstract changes in belief and membership of a faith community from the 'service' in question... [and] Faith participation is core to their identity and offer"; (2) *Half fat*, where "services are embedded with or delivered in close partnership with a worshipping community [and which] seek to offer and share faith and participation in the life of a worshipping community"; and (3) *Low fat*, which disavow proselytism or overt evangelism as such, but will see their service users on a spiritual journey on which they can assist, though in reactive ways."

45  Ben Ryan, *Catholic Social Thought and Catholic Charities in Britain Today: Need and Opportunity* (Theos, 2016) p. 43.

46  A number of forms – chaplaincy most obviously – are deliberately embedded in different structures, and while chaplains may make a virtue of persistence, relationships and local knowledge, they do not, of course, rely on the same embodied worshipping community in doing so. Indeed, it is precisely the chaplain's ability to be 'bilingual' – to speak the language of their faith and that of the institution in which they were placed – that gave them their strength. See Ben Ryan, *A Very Modern Ministry* (Theos, 2015).

47  And indeed way beyond, as one of the purposes behind the Torah was precisely, in the words of Deuteronomy 4:6, to "show your wisdom and understanding to the nations, who will hear about all these decrees and say, 'Surely this great nation is a wise and understanding people.'"

48  Geoff Knott, *Social Action and Church Growth* http://www.jubilee-plus.org/Publisher/File. aspx?ID=153728

49  There were one or two indications that this was also happening among Catholic churches, with regard to the activities of Catholic charities. Thus one interviewee told us that "all these community projects based out of parishes, they are really motivated, they are bringing people back into the church". However, this was not a commonly mentioned finding in this research, and the kind of evangelisation that was spoken of was much more along the lines of strengthening and deepening the existing faith of Catholics who participated in the action. See Ryan, *Catholic Charities*, p. 46.

50  Matthew 10:8

51  Benedict XVI, *Deus Caritas Est*, #31c; http://w2.vatican.va/content/benedict-xvi/en/ encyclicals/documents/hf_ben-xvi_enc_20051225_deus-caritas-est.html

52  Cf. Congregation for Bishops, Directory for the Pastoral Ministry of Bishops *'Apostolorum Successores'* (22 February 2004), 196, Vatican City 2004, p. 216.

53 For an overview of the study, see http://religionandsociety.org.uk/uploads/ docs/2012_10/1349188843_Johnsen_Phase_1_Small_Grant_Block.pdf

54 Paul Bickley, *The Problem of Proselytism* (Theos, 2015).

55 Bickley, *Proselytism*, p. 9. Emphases added.

56 If that disappoints some Christians who might hope for a more securely tangible bums-on-pews outcome, I would suggest they have misunderstood the nature of social liturgy (and possibly even of what conversion is). If it still disappoints them, however, it is possible that they might draw assurance from the findings of the Theos project into the social activity of Catholic charities in Britain. This found that Catholic charities were crucibles of "evangelisation", meaning not that they were places where non-Christians were 'converted' but rather where *existing Catholic spirituality was grown and deepened*. Time and again the research found that "charities served as crucibles of spirituality; building the spirituality of those who already considered themselves Catholics." This, once again, is not the end or objective of social liturgy. One does not run a club for the lonely or a clothing exchange scheme for those who can't afford new children's clothes in order to deepen one's own sense of God's love, any more than one does simply in order to increase congregation sizes. But it should be no surprise that living out the Christian faith in this concrete way does have the beneficial side-effect of deepening and strengthening one's faith.

57 They were able to get some funding from the Church Urban Fund "to establish a centre there [and] with the local church leaders… we were able to establish an advice centre that was a partnership between local people—the Muslim community as well as the Christian community—and the local authority."

58 Lord Ahmed, *Hansard*, 19 May 2006, Column 534.

59 On the differences between forms of secularism, in particular 'programmatic' and 'procedural', see Rowan Williams, *Faith in the Public Square* (Bloomsbury, 2012).

60 Richard Rorty, "Religion in the Public Square: A Reconsideration" in *The Journal of Religious Ethics*, Vol.31, No.1 (Spring, 2003), pp. 141-149.

61 Ben Clements and Nick Spencer, *Voting and Values: Does Religion Count?* (Theos, 2014); http://www.theosthinktank.co.uk/files/files/Reports/Voting%20and%20Values%20in%20Britain%20 12.pdf

62 Paul Bickley and Andrew Partington, *Coming off the bench: The past, present and future of religious representation in the House of Lords* (Theos, 2007).

63 Jonathan Chaplin, *Talking God: The Legitimacy of Religious Public Reasoning* (Theos, 2008).

64 Chaplin, *Talking God*, p. 1.